The
Classic Guide
to
RUGBY

The Classic Guide to RUGBY

D. R. Gent

AMBERLEY

First edition published 1922

This edition first published 2014

Amberley Publishing
The Hill, Stroud
Gloucestershire, GL5 4EP

www.amberley-books.com

British Library Cataloguing in Publication Data.
A catalogue record for this book is available from the British Library.

ISBN 978 1 4456 4478 3 (print)
ISBN 978 1 4456 4500 1 (ebook)

Typesetting and Origination by Amberley Publishing.
Printed in the UK.

Contents

Introduction

William Webb Ellis 'with fine disregard for the rules of football as played in his time at Rugby school, first took the ball in his arms and ran with it, thus originating the distinctive feature of the Rugby game'.

The question of where rugby began is a fiercely debated topic among historians. While the popular story of the schoolboy William Webb Ellis going rogue is an amusing anecdote, it is unlikely that the development of the game was sourced from one youngster's actions. 'Football' was played by a number of schools in the nineteenth century, including Eton, Harrow, Charterhouse, Westminster, Winchester, Shrewsbury and Rugby. The game played by these schoolboys has little resemblance to football or rugby as we now know it, but was more closely linked to riotous, Middle Age ball games with few rules. These early ball games were sometimes referred to as folk football, mob football or Shrovetide football and would usually be played between neighbouring towns or villages. Later banned, the purpose of these games was to move an inflated pig's bladder to markers at the end of the town by any means possible.

The lack of continuity between school games saw problems emerge when the schools played each other. The specific games each school had developed were fine within the context of each school's playing field, but as soon as games were played between each institution, chaos ensued. In one instance, in a game between Eton and Cambridge University, there was fierce disagreement when one boy picked up the ball and ran with it in his hands among those who were of the firm belief the ball should be kept on the floor. Reconciliation was eventually found in a 'compromise' game, which took the common rules played across the differing schools and eliminated the contentious elements.

The formation of the Football Association in 1863 saw an attempt to solidify one single game across the country to avoid future disagreements. Despite attempts by individual delegates and teams like Blackheath to mould the game according the Rugby School rules (tackling below the knee and running with the ball), the FA gradually moved away from handling laws and established 'soccer' as a game predominantly involving dribbling. This marked a distinctive separation between the two sports, and those supporting Rugby School rules continued to play their own very different rules removed from the FA. As the differences became increasingly more obvious, the RFU governing body was formed in 1871 and the distinction between rugby and football was cemented.

Written in 1922, *The Classic Guide to Rugby* looks at the shape of the game of rugby after the First World War. A firmly established and popular sport at the time of writing, D. R. Gent tackles differing types of play, the qualities of a good captain, the temperament required to be a patient and fair referee, the spirit of the game and rugby's position in future society. D. R. Gent had a successful rugby career himself in the early twentieth century, playing for Gloucester, Plymouth and England, and is therefore well placed to comment on the differing aspects of the game.

Gent's distaste for increasingly common features of the game like the disease of 'kicking mad' players, provides a humorous glimpse into concerns about the game in the past that are still echoed today. Society after the First World War was a turbulent place and, surprisingly, the concerns about the changing times are echoed in this guide to the game of rugby.

Hazel Cochrane
Editor

Preface

My object in writing this book has been to help people either to play Rugby or to appreciate it. During the years since the War, the interest displayed in the game has been greater than ever. But unfortunately, both with regard to the players and to the enthusiasm of the spectators, there often seems to be a lack of knowledge of the game. Keenness for a game is certainly the prime requisite, but the greater the knowledge that is possessed, the better for the game. For that reason, I hope that what I have written may conduce to a fuller enjoyment of Rugby by everybody who may happen to read it; and if it leads to a little less applause on the part of the spectators sometimes, for what is rank bad football, I shall feel not a little rewarded.

A word or two as to my "idea" of the book may be of assistance. The chapter headings will possibly mislead people. The last thing I should like to happen is for a full-back, let us say, to read the chapters on "full-back" play only, as he will then miss many points that concern his play. I have conceived the game as a whole, so that in order to get the fullest benefit that may accrue from the book, it is best to read it right through. That is one reason why I have made it so comparatively short, for the reading of fat tomes and the playing of Rugby do not always go hand in hand. The division into the chapters that I have chosen only implies that in those chapters are to be found the main points that crop up in connection with the various positions.

Throughout the book, readers will find continual reference to names of players who excelled at various phases of the game. These names have been chosen on two grounds only. First of all, I have included only the names of players I have actually played with, or of those whom I saw play when I could discriminate between good Rugby and bad. This means that many of the great "lights of other days" are not even mentioned; but this must not be interpreted as a lack of admiration for them on my part. I do admire them immensely, and realise what the game owes to them. Still, I consider it much more satisfactory to keep on the sure ground of personal experience than to use book knowledge, or to go by hearsay. Again, I have endeavoured – and a great task it has been – to refrain from reminiscence, except for the sole purpose of illustrating some aspect of the game. An intimate acquaintance with club, county, and international football for the past twenty years must needs have furnished one with a good deal of personal matter that would probably interest Rugby folk. I know, however, that had I succumbed to the temptation, there would have been precious little on how to play the game, and a vast amount about great names and games of the past twenty years. The absence of more reminiscences may disappoint some, but it would have been stretching the purpose of the book to include more.

July 1922.
D. R. GENT

OVERTAKEN

1

Forward Play (Part One)

Good forward play is undoubtedly the foundation of the Rugby Union game. A pack of forwards able to beat their opponents in close play and in the open will always beat a side whose backs are superior, provided the better pack is properly led. This last qualification is important, because so often are the better forwards badly led that their side loses, and the advantage of the superiority is at once questioned.

One instance in illustration of the truth of the statement will suffice. It was the match between France and Wales at Cardiff in 1921. The Frenchmen had a splendid set of backs, fast, nippy, and clever, whereas the Welsh backs were known to be poor in the extreme. T. Parker, the Welsh captain, and also the leader of the pack, knew the limitations of his backs and the strength of his opponents in that department, and went on the field with his tactics carefully thought out beforehand. He would make the game a forward one, and ignore his backs, except when he thought he could use them with safety. The plan worked admirably. By judicious heeling, wheeling, and close dribbling the game was completely "directed" by the Welsh forwards, and the Frenchmen, who had expected to win, were beaten with a fair amount of ease. Many other instances will come to the mind of anybody who has followed the game closely, and there is little doubt in my mind that had the Cambridge skipper of 1921 adopted these tactics, making the game a forward one (for his pack was much the better of the two), the Light Blues would have won that year's Varsity match. As it was, he reposed much more confidence in a weak set of backs than they deserved, and so Oxford won. It would have taken more than a good set of backs to beat a strong pack of forwards led by John Daniell (Cambridge and England), V. H. Cartwright (Oxford and England), W. Spiers (Devon), L. G. Brown (Blackheath and England), W. S. D. Craven (Blackheath), E. W. Roberts (Devon and England), T. Parker (Swansea and Wales), Mark Morrison (Royal High School and Scotland), or A. Tedford (Malone and Ireland), to name but a few good pack-leaders.

Forward play, then, being the basis of good Rugby, it is imperative that everybody should have a clear idea of what sound forward play is. But there is another reason. During the last ten or fifteen years, forward play has changed tremendously, and it now approximates closely to threequarter play in many respects. Previously, the main concern of a forward was his play in close work, *i.e.* scrummaging and dribbling. He was hardly expected to handle the ball with any certainty – that was the work of the backs. Now the pendulum has swung to the other extreme, and hard scrummaging and good dribbling are often ignored, the time being given to practice in developing passing and the ability to make openings. Consequently, the time seems opportune for a restatement of the principles of forward play.

SEVEN OR EIGHT FORWARDS

The rules say that there should be fifteen players on each side, but how they are to be arranged is left to the clubs themselves. For some years before the New Zealanders came here (in 1905) teams were arranged thus: eight forwards, two half-backs, four threequarters, and a full

PASSING AMONGST THE FORWARDS

back. The New Zealanders, however, played seven forwards (for scrum purposes), a "wing" forward (D. Gallaher), one half-back, two five-eighths, three threequarters, and a full back. As is well known, this fine team played havoc with our best sides, scoring 830 points as against 39, and people began to ask: "Is the arrangement of their men the cause of their superiority?"

The result was that many clubs modified their team-formation, especially with regard to the forwards. The change was short-lived, though, and most clubs reverted to the old formation. There are still just a few sides that cling to the seven forwards idea. I am all against it, as long as a side consists of fifteen players, my objection being that it needs clever play on the part of seven "out sides" not to get into each other's way, or to force the wing into touch: with eight "outsides" these tendencies are almost unavoidable, at least, with back play as stereotyped as it is to-day. Another objection is that the extra back militates against the development of individual play. There is precious little individualism as it is, without adding one more player to tempt others to pass instead of going on. Eight forwards, then, I shall consider as the number that constitutes the pack.

THE KICK-OFF AND DROP-OUT

Let us assume that your forwards are trained and are going to take part in a game. It is your kick-off, and the first point to consider is: where shall your forwards stand? The general custom now (there are a few exceptions, which will be noted later) is to kick the ball diagonally, to the right or to the left, roughly, in the direction of the "25" flag. The kicker has told the forwards to which side he is going to kick, and they should line-up on that side of him, the three fastest being nearest the touch-line, and the rest filling up the intervening space between them and the kicker. They should stand back a few yards from the centre line, and begin to run immediately after the kicker has started, so that they pass the line as soon as possible after the ball has been kicked, and well under way when they reach the centre line. Their objective is the ball; or, as more often happens, the man about to field the ball; but the former is the ideal to have in mind. Obviously, if the ball has been kicked truly, the three fast men on the extreme left (or right, as the case may be) stand the best chance of getting to the ball, not only because they are the fastest men, but also because they have the shortest distance to travel. These three should make their run up with the fastest in the middle, and the other two about a couple of yards on either side of him. Then, if the fielder of the ball is bold enough to try to make some ground before he puts in his kick, he will find his way barred by these three near the touch-line, and by the other four (or five, if a back has kicked off) in the middle of the field. The three who are going for the man must watch him very carefully, and, as they approach him, pull up slightly, so that they have themselves under better control if they have to tackle their opponent. It is very difficult indeed to beat three men coming up to you, the middle one slightly ahead, and the other two just a few yards away from him on either side. Kicks-off are far too carelessly taken; if a man who worked with his fastest forwards on the plan just outlined was entrusted with these kicks, his side would often benefit greatly by a kick-off , instead of being sent back forty or fifty yards by a good return kick. Too often, nowadays, anyone takes the kick-off, and he kicks it without any definite plan.

Now, having followed up closely, there are a few alternatives before the forwards. They may be fortunate and reach the ball before an opponent. In that case, if the ball comes to hand comfortably – a rare occurrence – the nearest forward should catch it and start a bout of short passing, or put the ball down quickly and start a dribble; which he does, will depend on the state of the ground or the ability of his forwards to handle. The safer plan would be to start a dribble, always assuming, of course, that the man in possession is unable to go any further. It would be absurd to pass or put the ball down for a dribble when the man in possession could make headway, and perhaps score with a display of cleverness, speed, or dash. Rarely, however, is the kick so well placed as to enable the following-up forward to get possession.

If an opponent fields the ball, the game is to get to him quickly, and if you can lay hands on him before he kicks, to bring him down hard – not foully, but vigorously, – and to hold him there, so that he doesn't get away. Having got him down, make him play the ball, by which time your men should have gathered round, and should be bustling the tackled man to make him let the ball go, so that you can start a concerted dribble. There is one other alternative: your opponent may see you approach, and, realising that it is hopeless to try to break through, he may elect to kick to touch at once, timing it to get in his kick just before you reach him. Then be prepared to charge his kick down. Jump towards the flight of the ball, protecting your face with your hands; and if the ball does rebound off you without "winding" you or otherwise hurting you, you will be well placed, for the ball will sail towards your opponents' goal-line, possibly with you close behind it. If your side kicks off, then, keep these alternatives before you as you follow up. If forwards are slack in following up, or follow up without a system, an opponent is often able to return the ball thirty or forty yards behind the original kicker, and nothing disheartens forwards more than to follow up, and then to have to drag back, perhaps double the distance, to take part in a line-out or a scrum.

Suppose the other side kicks off. From the disposition of your opponents, you can infer which way the kick is likely to go, and a forward's duty then is to help to fill up the quarter in which the ball will probably drop. This is often carelessly done: fellows seem to get anywhere. Gauge the probable length of the kick and take up a position, the ideal arrangement being one where the quarter in question is dotted with players much about the same distance apart. Should the ball come directly to a forward he should field it cleanly, and decide in a flash whether he is going to make a dash on his own, pass to a back, who may be able to start a good attack, kick to touch, or drop the ball and start a dribble. Which he should do will depend on circumstances. The alternative most frequently chosen is the kick to touch; but it is one to be avoided unless the forward is very hard pressed.

The plan least often adopted is that of passing back, and yet, with a good set of backs, this is the most likely way of benefiting by your opponents' kick-off. Did not Wales lose to England in 1910 at the opening of the Twickenham ground mainly through this manoeuvre? Wales kicked off (to begin the match) and the ball went to our captain, Adrian Stoop – not a forward, of course, but standing, just then, well among the forwards. He at once made off into the open, and following some skilful passing F. E. Chapman scored far out. The same player converted, and we were five points up before the crowd had realised almost that the match had started, though the welkin rang when they did realise it! Should the following-up be done properly, and, consequently, cause you to have no time to kick, pass, or run, all you can do is to throw the ball down at your own feet and try to dribble away, receiving the support of the rest of your pack as soon as they can get to you, which is immediately, for they should have bunched around you when it was obvious that the ball was going to you.

Almost the same procedure takes place after a drop-out, with this difference: the following-up forwards should rarely, if ever, allow their opponents to return the ball. Being a drop-kick, the kicker can put more height into it, and so give his forwards a shorter distance to run, to the greater discomfiture of his opponents.

DRIBBLING

This surely is one of the lost arts of English Rugby, though one still sees it occasionally in Scottish and Irish games, whilst the Welsh pack showed at Cardiff in 1922, when they routed England, that they, too, had not quite forgotten how to dribble. The sooner this lost art is recaptured in England the better for the game, and it is sincerely to be hoped that in every Public School where the game is being taught, and in every other club for that matter, plenty of time and thought will be given to teaching players, especially forwards, how to dribble. For one thing, it is an integral part of traditional English Rugby – no small recommendation. Again, it is one of the recognised means of attack and defence; in addition to which, though this is a minor reason, dribbling done properly appeals almost as much to the spectators as good passing. In fact, what more exhilarating sight can you have than that of a stalwart pack of forwards tearing down the field, with the ball admirably under control and being passed from man to man whilst their opponents are being brushed aside or bowled over like ninepins?

Though the forwards should be the expert dribblers of the team, every other member should also practise this art, especially the scrum half, who often, particularly on a wet ground, will have plenty of dribbling to do. The most important part of dribbling is "ball-control." You may have the best intentions in the world, but if in your dribble you

A DRIBBLE— ALL BY HIMSELF.

miskick and send the ball more than about a yard from you, you will generally find that a nippy opponent will quickly gather it and either dodge past you (for as you are going at a fair pace, it will be difficult to tackle anybody going in the opposite direction) or kick well over your head. A forward must learn to control the ball – that is fundamental. He should strive, by incessant practice, to run at a steady pace (about half-speed) and keep the ball all the time not more than a yard away from him. To do this, he must never use his toes; the outside of the foot is the part to use, recourse being had occasionally to the inside of the foot and the instep. Set out to master ball-control with the outside of the foot, always remembering that there are times when it is more convenient in your stride to use the other parts named.

Let any player who has never done so before take a Rugby ball out on his own and try a dribble, seeing how far he can go, whilst keeping the ball within the prescribed distance. He will soon realise how much there is to learn before he can call himself a good dribbler. To a beginner I should suggest that he begin his practice by going at a walking pace almost, and then slowly to increase his pace, as he acquires a mastery over the ball. All the time you are dribbling you will find that you must watch the ball intently, for, owing to its being such a weird shape (from a dribbling point of view), you must see exactly what part of it you are going to tap, for that will affect the whole nature of the tap. In a match, of course, you also must glance at the opposition, so as to know how to beat anybody, whether by going one side of him yourself, or by a pass to one of your side.

The expert dribbler in Rugby is always the fellow who has given hours to practice, or the one who has played Association and has learnt to adapt himself to the oval ball. My advice to any forward is to spend plenty of time in learning to dribble. With regular skipping to give you strength in the balls of your feet, and plenty of perseverance, any player who is not flat-footed should become a good dribbler. I have known many a player get his place in a side largely because he could dribble well. In every club that I have captained or had much to do with, I have insisted on a great part of the training time of a forward being given to dribbling practice. A favourite plan of mine was to spend about a quarter of an hour in a game between the backs and the forwards, playing a kind of Association with a Rugby ball, across half the field, with the half-way line and a goal-line as our touch-lines. It is quite easy to devise a set of rules that will enable this to be done.

So far I have had in mind dribbling by an individual. Now let us consider for a moment concerted dribbles. When a number of forwards start off on one of these dribbles, they should not spread out too far. The best formation is for the leader of the dribble – in other words, the man who starts it – to have one man on each side of him, to whom he can pass, if necessary, and a couple about two or three yards behind, ready to take up the dribble should one of the men in front over-run the ball, and also ready to check the progress of an opponent if he should rob your man of the ball and himself attempt to come through. The man in possession of the ball when these dribbles are in progress must be wide-awake, too, for all the time he must be aware of the position of his opponents, the ball, and his "supporters", in the dribble, whilst if he himself over-runs the ball he must at once side-step to his right or left, to leave room for his "supporters" to come through. The outsides should also keep up with a concerted dribble – or some of them, at all events. Many a try has been scored by a back supporting a dribble wide out, and then getting a long pass forward (with the foot) into a spot where the outside has been able to field quickly and to cross the line. Such tactics as these can easily be worked out theoretically off the field, and put into practice with great effect.

Another thing to be remembered in dribbling is the effect of a heavy ground. On a hard, fiery ground the least tap will send the ball quite a long way, so that you have to be very careful indeed not to kick too hard. When the ground is heavy, on the other hand, this gentle tap is useless; you will find that you over-run the ball every time. The ball must be kicked with quite a lot of force to keep it the required distance from you. It was failure to recognise this fact that was largely responsible for the debacle at Cardiff in 1922, when England was so badly beaten by Wales. There were some splendid dribblers in the English pack, but time and time again they would go off with a concerted dribble, and over-run the ball, only to have the chagrin of seeing the Welsh forwards, led by T. Parker, come through and take up the dribble themselves. A skilled forward should get the speed of a ball after ten minutes' play, if the climatic conditions remain the same.

To sum up these notes on dribbling, then: ball control is the main factor, the outside of the foot is the part to be used, and the ball must never get more than a yard away. A man should begin by practising to dribble at a slow pace, and work up to half speed; he must keep his eyes on the ball, opponents, and "supporters"; and, finally, he must try to get the weight of the ball as quickly as he can.

2

Forward Play (Part Two)

THE LINE-OUT

Let us assume that it is your "line," *i.e.* your half has to throw the ball in. Your leader will probably have chosen one man, or perhaps two, tall and with safe hands, to stand at the farther end of the line, so that if either of these men is unmarked, or marked by a short man, the ball may be thrown to him, in the hope that he will set the backs going, or go through on his own. The rest will generally spread themselves out to fill the intervening space between the men in the long line and the touch-line. Your half should then glance down the line before throwing the ball in, to see what player stands the best chance of taking it. We will suppose that you make a fair catch; what are you to do? Well, there are many alternatives:

1. You can pass the ball swiftly to your outside half or centre, who will be in your rear, and so set the backs in motion. To do this properly requires a lot of practice, for a forward is apt to throw the ball too hard, or with bad direction. This is nearly always dangerous to your side, for the opposing forwards can easily dash through and set up an attack or clear their lines, as the case may be, since your men have to turn round to reach the ball, whereas they have simply to run straight ahead. Plenty of practice, however, will soon enable a forward to get into the way of giving this overhead pass, with the right strength and in

A THROW OUT OF TOUCH

the right direction. I have seen many splendid tries scored by a set of backs who have received the ball by a swift oblique pass from a line-out. A slight variation of this is not to actually field the ball, but to deflect it in its course with the palm of the hand, towards one of your backs. This is an extremely difficult thing to do, but it is wonderfully effective if well done, as much valuable time can be saved by not having to catch the ball and pass it again, and also because one can get such a lot of pace by this "flick," as it were. I again caution any forward, however, to be chary of using this method unless he is sure of himself, and his backs are aware of what he is going to do, for, on their part, a ball passed from the line-out in this way takes a lot of fielding. I remember the Newport teams of 1906–10 working this trick admirably.

2. There may be a chance to go right through on your own. Theoretically this seems impossible: there are eight forwards on either side, and they should pair off and mark each other. But in practice this is frequently possible. How often does one hear the captain shout out, "Mark your man there!" simply because his fellows have forgotten their duty in the line-out? You must be on the look out for this, and, if there is half a chance, you should slip unostentatiously into the unmarked spot, and hope that your half will see you. Dozens of tries have been scored in this way, as a result of watchfulness on the part of the half and the forward. If you do get possession like this, go through with all the dash and speed you can command.

3. You can throw the ball down at your own feet and start a dribble, or you can throw it sideways to a colleague not so well marked as you are, and then back him up in the dribble he has started.

4. If you are on the defence, you can punt to touch. But you must be very careful to find touch, or you will only give your opponents what they want, *viz*. the chance of setting

up an attack by open play. This kicking must only be done, then, by a fairly safe kick.

Which of these alternatives you adopt will depend upon how you are placed and what your strong points are.

Sometimes, however, especially if a side is on the defence, the forwards will be ordered by their leader to "bunch up," *i.e.* about five of them will get close together in the line-out, five yards or so from the touch-line. Then the half will throw the ball into the midst of them, in the hope that one of his men will take it, drop it at his feet, and relieve the situation by a very solid sort of dribble towards the touch-line, the men practically touching each other. Often this "bunching-up" in the line out is used as a blind, for, whilst four or five forwards are closing together in this way, a couple of fast men will quietly ease off to the end of the line, and receive a long pass from the half.

Another trick in the line-out is to let your forwards get well out for a long line, leaving a space between the first forward and the touch-line of anything from five to ten yards. As none of your forwards are there, it is more than likely that your opponents will not defend that opening, and there will be an excellent chance for your wing to dash through this gap, receive a swift pass from your half, and score.

If your half is not throwing in, your object is clear: you must mark a man. It may be somebody that you have been told to mark all through the match, which often happens; but you must mark somebody. As I have just said, it seems a quite unnecessary piece of advice to give, but I will guarantee that in half of the lines-out one sees, there is somebody unmarked. Now should the ball be thrown to your opponent, there are one or two things you can do. You must certainly jump for the ball as it approaches him, so that if possible you get it, and not he. But should he make the catch, you must smother him and the ball. This is one of the rare occasions when a high tackle is correct. As he takes the ball, get your arms round his, preferably near the shoulders, and so make him powerless to part with the ball. At the same time, grip him so firmly as to prevent his flinging you off from his shoulders. The danger about tackling him low is that he might still have the chance of parting with the ball to his side's advantage, which will make your tackle less effective than it should have been. If you can't get at his arms simultaneously with his taking the ball, go for him low, and get him down quickly, so that he will have very little time in which to pass. I shall have something to say in a later chapter about refereeing, but it is relevant to say here that it is in the lines-out that one sees more dirty work that escapes punishment than anywhere else. Charging an opponent before he is actually in possession is far too common, whilst the throwing in of the ball by the half-back just a wee bit out of the straight and in the direction of the opponents' goal-line enables his forwards to slip through and take the ball behind their opponents, which places the latter at a tremendous disadvantage. So weak have many referees been that I have seen this trick carried on successfully all through a match, even an international match.

Another bad feature of many lines-out, though I don't call this unfair, so much as brainless, is the frequency with which one sees a forward of the side not throwing out of line, jump and simply hit the ball away anywhere. I suppose these players work on this principle: anything is good that prevents your opponents from getting the ball. The practice seems to me to be ridiculous: if you can hit it, why not try to make a fair catch? Too often, I am afraid, it is due to lack of pluck: a forward is afraid to take the ball himself with the chances of a hard tackle, so he keeps it away from an opponent. A variation of this practice, countenanced alike by some referees and some captains, to my surprise, is for a forward to stand close to the touch-line and do his best to prevent the half from making a good throw-in. More than once this has become quite farcical, the half feinting to throw in, and the forward bobbing up and down like a Jack-in-the-box. The procedure is useless, and no captain should allow it to happen twice in a game. If a forward is told off to mark the short line, his duty is to keep his eyes on his opponents, not to go through the antics just described.

Forwards who wish to shine in the line-out, then, must practice:

1. Taking the ball in the air by a well-timed jump.
2. Giving fairly swift, but very straight, passes to players behind them, or on either side of them.
3. Dropping the ball and dribbling off smartly.
4. Tackling a man in such a way that he comes to earth and the ball is smothered as well.
5. Using their eyes to find the best position to take up; and
6. Most important of all, they must mark some body when the other side is throwing in.

SCRUMMAGING

How many ways it is possible for eight men to form a scrummage I leave the mathematician to decide. Certain it is, however, that how these eight can pack to the best advantage is a question discussed whenever Rugby forwards get together. It seems a veritable King Charles's head with some people – the very mention of Rugby starts a discussion on scrum-formation. Much interesting matter have I read and heard about it; but my own opinion is that far too much is made of it, and the theory of this subject has outrun the practice. Consequently I am not going to discuss any but the normal 3-2-3 and 3-3-2 formations. Both these formations have had their advocates for years, and there is a good deal to be said for both; but I prefer the first of the two, *viz.* the 3-2-3 formation. The following diagram will show the respective formations: –

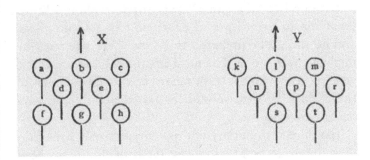

The diagram will make clearer my preference for the 3-2-3 (X) formation, these being my reasons : –

I. The scrum is more compact, and the pushing can better be done towards the centre.

2. The flank men in the third row ("f" and "h") are much more easily able to break away from the scrum and join in the attack or defence, as the case may be. As their assistance has almost become an integral part of modern Rugby, this is a very important reason.

It is not so good as the 3-3-2 formation for wheeling purposes, obviously, for the third man in the second row is so valuable for wheeling. If you are going to wheel to the right, you will have this third man ("r") on the right, as in the figure; if to the left he will get down on the left (moving to the left of "n").

But without going too fully into this matter, as it admits of endless argument, I plump for the 3-2-3 formation as the basis of packing in the scrummage. Some have advocated a mixture of both, adopting the 3-3-2 when you are going to wheel. But suppose you don't get possession? You are then robbed of the advantage of the two flankers in the rear rank.

Shall the forwards have set places? No, I say. Too often the game is slowed down a good deal whilst men are taking their set places. Besides, I consider too much specialising is not good for the game. Every forward should know what the functions are of every unit in a scrummage, and he should be prepared to do his share wherever he might happen to be. The most notable exception to this general utility idea is with regard to the outside men of the third row, who should, as far as possible, always occupy that position.

The three men in the front row are primarily hookers – their duty is to be able to divert the ball, after it has been thrown in by the half, to their own side of the scrummage, and that with either foot. The first man up – and the best hooker in the pack should try to get this position – should take up his position with arms outstretched, ready for the next two forwards to come up. They should line up on either side of him, not both on one side, and when all three have locked, *i.e.* the middle man has been firmly gripped by the other two, high up under the arm-pits, they should pack low, with their legs well back. This locking will result in the middle man being slightly in front of his flank men, as he should be, for it is a decided advantage to have your chief hooker "up" a little. To make quite sure that you get this advantage, the flankers must bind their inner arms round the centre man underneath his own arms, though as high up as possible.

Then come the two men of the second rank ("d" and "e" of X), who should be the strongest forwards on the side, for they are the locks of the scrum as a whole. They pack with their shoulders just below the hips of the two men in front of each of them, heads well down, legs well back, not bunched up under them, and gripping each other very firmly with the inner arm, whilst their outer arm should be round the waist of the flank man of the front row.

The middle man of the third row ("g" in the diagram) should also, be a strong forward, as his function is very similar to that of the two second row men. The two outside men of the third row ("f" and "h") are in a different category. They should be fast, and able to take part in a "back" movement, whilst they should keep an eye on the opposing halves should the ball go to the other side of the scrum, and be ready to nip their play in the bud. As I intend discussing wing forward play in the next chapter, I will leave this subject for the moment. You have now your scrum formed, three clever men at hooking in front, two strong men in the next row, a "pusher" and two flank men in the third row, but all capable of taking up any position in the scrum, with a knowledge of the requirements of that position. As they go down all these men should pack low, with their eyes open, and their legs well back, for no proper "shoving" can be done with the legs at right angles to the body, or with the eyes shut.

Now the ball is going in – on the left side, we will say. As the outside man ("a") in the front row cannot touch the ball until it has passed him, all he can do to start with is to watch the ball, and to keep pushing hard. The centre man ("b") is the one to get the ball, generally speaking, and in this case he should swing his right foot round and guide the ball with a sharp oblique tap towards his side of the scrummage. The outside man on the left side ("a") should by then have swung his left foot towards the centre and aided the middle man to get the ball through the space between their two inner legs. The support of the outside man is necessary, for otherwise the tendency is for the centre man to kick the ball out to the half again. "d" and "e" will be pushing and watching all the time, and if the ball is obtained by their frontrank men, they must make room for it to pass through the middle of the scrum, by keeping their legs well apart, or by raising their inner legs and so not impeding its progress. Sometimes they may have to give it a gentle tap themselves towards the space between "f" and "g," if it hangs a bit. Again "d" and "e" must be very careful to see that the ball does not leave the scrummage at the side, between them and "a" or "c," or between them and "f" or "g," for this will often enable the opposing scrum half to gain possession, their own scrum half being in the rear of the scrummage. The middle man of the third row ("g") has an important position, for which reason this is an ideal position for a pack-leader to take up. He has to decide whether the ball is to go out or not. The opposing half may be right on top of his own half, and nothing would be gained by letting the ball go out. "g" will then decide, doubtless, to keep the ball in and wheel. It may be asked, how can "g" tell what is the position behind him? He must practise looking down and between his own and the flankers' legs, so as to be able to recognise his own scrum half by his stockings or his legs. In addition, the scrum half may give him the signal by word of mouth or by a gentle tap, that he wishes the ball kept in. If the ball is to go out, "g" and the flank men ("f" and "h") will either leave an avenue for the ball to pass through, or if it hasn't enough way on, will heel it gently to the half, who should receive it either from the opening between "f" and "g," or between "g" and "h," or between "g's" legs.

Oh, this last *gentle* tap! I was an inside half practically all my playing days, and the times the ball has reached me like a shot out of a gun, when it has been impossible to pick it up and pass it; or when some huge forward has back-heeled like a donkey to kick me hard in the face or on the hands! Dentists' bills, broken finger-joints, and disfigured features have been the penalties I have had to pay. As these were done by my own side, I will presume that they meant well! But what an abuse of keenness! In addition to my own discomfort and chagrin, I have seen my side let down badly

A SCRUMMAGE

dozens of times. A mighty back-heel has sent the ball yards towards our own goal-line (generally to an unmarked spot), and a try has been the result. Thus it will be seen that there is a great art in heeling, an art not confined to the hookers, but one affecting every member of the pack. Here it cannot be emphasised too strongly that, except for the second or so that you are actually heeling the ball yourself, you must be pushing towards the centre of the scrum with all your might. If you don't do this, your side will probably lose possession by being pushed off the ball.

For the moment, we will assume that you are heeling to feed your backs, so won't concern ourselves with getting possession to wheel. As soon as the ball is clear of the scrummage the pack must break up at once. The flankers, especially the one on the side to which the ball has gone, will join in the attack, ready to take the inside pass or kick across that may come along. As soon as they can, the rest of the pack will spread out across the field in the direction of the play, and be prepared for any emergency – a tackle, a dribble, a pass, or what not. In addition, it is a good plan for a forward with a safe pair of hands, and able to kick reasonably well, to drop back towards the other side of the field from where his full back is standing, for fear a kick down the field by an opponent may transfer play to that quarter. Again, two or three forwards should make straight for the goal-posts, ready to take the punt across that your wing will ball at his feet, and lead the dribble in the second stage of the wheel. As soon as the front rank have heeled the ball back, they should immediately divert their pushing towards the left, and push harder than ever. This is imperative, as upon this depends the success of the manoeuvre. Simultaneously with the front-rank push towards the left, the other five men must, whilst pushing all the time, veer round towards the right. If this is done properly the pack in possession should be able to wheel the scrummage until the line of the scrummage is across the field, instead of up and down the field. But just before the scrummage is dead across the field, the second stage of the wheel should begin. The right-hand man of the second rank is the important person here. He must break away from the scrummage with the ball at his feet, and with the two back-row men who packed on either side of him, in support. These three should dash up the field in a concerted dribble, and the other forwards of the second and third rank should join in the dribble as soon as possible. Whilst these five are engaged in the first stages of this dribble, the front rank must keep down and push hard all the time. The great danger in this stage is that the forwards, in their keenness to break away and start the dribble, will leave the ball behind them or lose it almost immediately; to avoid this, those in support of the leader of the dribble should follow him, one on either side, and slightly behind him, and the other two right behind him, so as to carry on the dribble if he should over-run the ball.

Often it is a good plan to relieve your line by a wheel. Suppose your opponents are attacking and have forced you to a position near your goal-line and close to the touch-line. It is an effective way to ease the situation by wheeling the scrum towards the touch-line. This will probably result in a gain of ten yards or so, and keep the ball at the same time from the opposing backs; but even this must not be done as a matter of course, for if the opposing forwards are particularly good in the line-out, you are giving them a splendid opportunity, as your wheel will almost certainly lead to a throwin for them. Still, this is the normal use of a wheel, *viz.* to clear one's lines by keeping the ball towards the touch-line, and by gaining a little ground at the same time. When a side is superior in scrummage work, however, wheeling may frequently be used to advantage for offensive as well as for defensive purposes.

To check a wheel, the obvious thing is to try to keep up your push in the contrary direction to what your opponents wish you to go. This is difficult, and rarely of much avail, though it must always be attempted. But when you see that your opponents have got their swing well under way, the outside men of your rear rank should double round the scrum towards the head of the prospective dribble and pack in against the ball, thus blocking the dribble. A wheel well-executed is a very fine feature of the game, and if the wheel itself is also well-timed it can be most useful to a side. Nothing like enough is made of wheeling nowadays.

THE "WING" FORWARD

"Winging" is, comparatively speaking, a modem feature of the game, and its introduction has done infinitely more harm than good. As I was always an inside half myself, and consequently the prey for all "wingers" of my time, the "wing" forward was always my *bête noir*, so I may be prejudiced; but, for what it is worth, I do emphatically declare that the game of Rugby has suffered sadly by the systematic playing of a forward (or, what is far commoner nowadays, *some* forwards) for the main purpose of winging. As I write this, I am fully conscious of the clever work of such brilliant players as Charles Fillman and A. T. Voyce for England, Ivor Morgan for Wales, G. H. Maxwell for Scotland, and, the greatest of them all, though the originator of the idea, W. Spiers, for many years captain of Devon Albion and Devon County, and a contemporary of Commander E. W. Roberts, R.N., the old Devon and English forward, and a member of the English Selection Committee in 1921 and 1922.

The game, as conceived by Spiers, was for the wing forward, when his side was on the defence, or in opposition to a strong back division, to get quickly among his

SCREWING THE SCRUMMAGE.

opponents when the ball came out their side, and nip the passing movement in the bud. For this purpose he either did not go down into the scrummage, or, what was more often the case, he would take his place on the outside and in the rear of the pack. With his wonderful knowledge of the game, and his uncanny instinct for the development of an attack, he was nearly always either on top of the man with the ball or in close proximity to the man who was going to get it next. If, on the other hand, the ball came out on his side, he was brilliantly able to join in the attack. I have seen him side-step, feint, and burst through, as skilfully as any but the very best of threequarters, whilst he had another favourite trick that was almost certain to get him past his opponents. That was to pass the ball with the right hand, say, across the body, apparently to someone on his left, and then to stop it with his left hand, regain possession (though he actually had never lost it), and side-step past his opponents. The only modern forward I have seen do this trick with any success is H. L. Price, the Oxford and England player.

The New Zealanders had a recognised "winger," *viz.* their captain, David Gallaher; but his conception of "winging" was different from Spiers's. Gallaher never went into the scrummage: as a matter of fact, he always put the ball in, leaving the only half-back (generally F. Roberts) to stand at the base of the scrum ready to feed his five-eighths. Their wonderful success caused the "All Blacks" to be imitated in all sorts of ways; "wing" forwards became the order of the day, and, unfortunately, they have been with us ever since.

I will grant that a "wing" forward who knows his peculiar functions well, who has the temperament and physical ability to carry out these functions properly, and who will steadfastly endeavour to resist the temptation to which I shall refer in a minute, can be a most useful member of a side. Charles Fillman proved that during the dozen or so years that he played for Blackheath and England; and as one who was continually in opposition to him, I should like to record the fact that I consider Fillman the fairest "wing" forward I have ever seen or played against.

But my great objection to "winging" is that it nearly always degenerates into nothing but systematic obstruction. Any method that keeps the opposing scrum half from coming round to interfere with your scrum half is fair to the "winger." Sometimes, the "wing" forward will throw his leg out from the scrum (if he has gone into the pack) and trip the scrum half (on the blind side of the referee, of course): sometimes he will get between his own two halves, ostensibly to join in the movement, but really for no other purpose than to block the other half as he comes up to take the outside half – a subtle form of obstruction this; and there are many other forms of obstruction that this particular player indulges in, most of which escape the notice of the crowd, and generally that of the referee as well. Ask any scrum half you know, though especially one in first-class football, and he will soon enlighten you as to what unfair tactics go on round about the scrummage, thanks to these unscrupulous "wingers." Since the War the evil has, if anything, been aggravated, for " winging " has become by far the most popular aspect of forward play, and has been indulged in by dozens of forwards who had not the faintest notion of their duty, except that it was to obstruct the opposing half, or to get offside when their opponents looked dangerous.

My advice to any school, then, is to discourage "winging" in every possible way. I should make a boy play in one of the four recognised positions. If he is to be a forward, he should be taught the conventional forward game, with frequent reminders that "winging" is a sure road to being dropped. In first-class football it is rather different, and if you have a man with the right temperament, and the physical ability, he might certainly be allowed to develop his play on fair "winging" lines. But I call to mind many clubs whom I hated to play against on account of the foul tactics of the recognised "wing" forward of the side. The position was not made any the more comfortable by the fact that obstruction by "wing" forwards nearly always meant a big man versus a little man.

The "wing" forward who plays his game properly should be able to join in the attack if the ball comes out his side, should be nimble enough to get on top of his opponents if they should get possession, should have a fine sense of anticipation whether in attack or defence, should be a good rush-stopper – for he will often have to check forward rushes, and should have a good turn of speed and a safe pair of hands. In short, he should possess most of the qualities of a centre three quarters, together with the physique of a lightish forward. Above all, however, he should have the right temperament, or, to put it quite bluntly, he should be able to resist the very strong temptation to obstruct – one of the worst fouls in the game, if done with intent. A side – be it club, county, or country – that persists in playing a "winger" who revels in the seamy side of "winging" is tolerating a practice that is not in keeping with the best traditions of the Rugby Union game. I have spoken strongly of this aspect of forward play because I believe that the game is often spoilt as a spectacle by brainless "winging," and that a nasty spirit is very frequently introduced into the games of to-day largely owing to the doubtful tactics of these "disappointed threequarters."

THE "LOOSE HEAD"

A few words on this subject should fittingly follow what has been said about "winging," for the "loose-head" idea is another curse of the game. Though it was not introduced then for the first time, it was the visit of the New Zealanders in 1905 that established this practice, when the Welsh players, always great students of the game off the field as well as on, devised a means whereby they could prevent their opponents from getting possession; and, to be candid, it is in Wales that the practice has become commonest. The "loose head" is a term well known in the Rugby world, but what it means is nothing like so well known. The accompanying diagram will show at a glance what it means. "A," "B," and

"C" are the three front-row forwards of one side; "X," "Y," and "Z" of another. When they pack, one man on each side has his head practically free. "A" and "Z" are the men in the above diagram. The heads of "B," "C," "X," and "Y" are locked. Now the rule says that the ball is not really in the scrummage until it has passed the two outside men of the front rank. If the ball is thrown in from direction "R," it is "C" and "Z" who are put out of action *pro tem.*; if it is from direction "L," it is "A" and "X" who are put out of action. Suppose the ball is thrown in from "R"; the "X," "Y," "Z" side has a great advantage, for the principal hooker ("Y") is much nearer the ball than the principal hooker of the other side ("B"); whilst if it should pass "B" and "Y" there is yet "X," who will have a better chance of trapping the ball than "A." Similarly, if the ball is thrown in from "L," the same advantages will accrue to the "A," "B," "C" side.

In our diagram, when the ball comes in on the "R" side, the "X," "Y," "Z" forwards are said to have the loose head; "Z's" being the loose head referred to. When it comes in on the "L" side, "A," "B," "C" have the loose head; "A's" head being the loose one. Obviously it is an advantage to have this loose head, and it is the art of packing so that a side can get this advantage that has led to what are known as "loose-head" tactics, which, unfortunately, are to be met with in even International football. In its worst form it means that if the ball is coming in from the "R" side, "A" doubles round to the left of "C," giving his side the loose head. Then round comes "X" to the right of "Z," and so on, with the probable chance that the third-row men will also join in this merry-go-round. I have seen as many as six men up in the front row on each side, with the ball still in the half's hand!

The new rule, adopted by the Rugby Union in 1922, should reduce considerably the amount of trouble this wretched practice causes. By this rule, it is illegal to have more than three men in the front row of a properly constituted "tight" scrummage, as opposed to a loose one, so that the running round just referred to should well-nigh cease. Fortunately, however, a lot is still left to the sportsmanship of the players, as it will even now be possible for a side that is more concerned with the letter of the law than its spirit to start "loose-head" tactics. The first-row forwards of a side should try, when they go down, to get the "loose head," for they know before they go down, on which side the ball is coming in generally, at all events. If in the packing, however, the other fellows get the "loose head," you must rest content with endeavouring to hook the ball away from your opponents, despite this "loose head" advantage. To counteract the tactics that are likely to be used, despite the new rule, I think referees should allow the loose head to go either to the side that first had their three front-row men down (this will defeat the tendency to have two down to start with, and a third ready to move up on the "loose-head" side, from the second row probably), or to the side that did not cause the stoppage that led to the scrummage. It is to be hoped that referees will apply this new rule firmly and fairly. Again, though, I would insist upon the great responsibility of captains in this respect. They should endeavour to instil into their sides the give-and-take nature of the "loose-head" business, and then, with that feeling and the new powers applied to referees, we ought to see the gradual elimination of a practice that has eaten deeply into the spirit of the game.

Sound forward play, as I said to begin with, is the basis of good Rugby. The different aspects of forward play are not too well known, judging by what one sees nowadays. I have tried to point out a few of the duties of a forward, in the hope that any players who may chance to read what I have written may build their game on foundations that are, I believe, in keeping with the best traditions of the game, and are yet suited to the some what modified form of the game that has been evolved during the last fifteen years or so. I will venture to say that half the forward play one has seen during the past season or two has been unworthy of the name, mainly because it was so hybrid in its nature. I do not like naming prominent players of to-day, but no player I have seen for the past two years has so well carried out what I conceive to be the proper functions of a forward as W. W. Wakefield, the English International and Cambridge captain. I commend anyone who wants to see standard forward play at its best to go and watch Wakefield for a time or two.

3
Half-Back Play (Part One)

It is of immense value to a side to possess a good pair of halves. In post-War football this has been amply demonstrated by the play of the brilliant English pair, Lieut.-Commander W. J. A. Davies, R.N., and Lieut. C. A. Kershaw, R.N. The magnificent play of either or both must have won at least a dozen games for the United Services, the Royal Navy, and England, when their side has been beaten in every other phase of the game. It was the same for some time before the War, when that glorious player the late Lieut. F. E. Oakley partnered Davies: the same clubs had a tremendous pull over all-comers by virtue of having good players at half. Think, too, what assets to their side were "Pat" Munro and the late E. D. Simson (Scotland), Louis Magee and J. J. Coffey (Ireland), R. M. Owen and R. Jones (Wales), H. W. Carolin and F. J. Dobbin (South Africa), and Adrian Stoop and Munro (Oxford), to name but a few great pairs of halves. These, I know, were all great players, and it may be contended that two great players in any side, if playing together, may make an otherwise bad side do well. This is quite true, but nowhere does it apply so much as at half-back. Again, a bad pair of halves will ruin any side. However well your forwards may perform, unless they are reasonably well supported by the halves, they will need more than a little luck to drive home their attacks to the extent of scoring. And the threequarters, of course, are in a hopeless plight if they are not fed properly, for the chances that reach the "threes" other than through the half-backs are few and far between.

Time was when the two half-backs worked more on individualistic lines than they do now. My first partner for Gloucestershire (in 1904) was W. V. Butcher (Richmond and England), and we always took half the field each for the purpose of working the scrum, and throwing in from touch. I took the left of the field, and he the right. Whenever there was a scrummage on the right side of the field, he put the ball in, and I took the outside position; on the left side it was *vice versa*. With most English sides at that time that was the custom, though, as a matter of fact, it did not prevail with my own club (Gloucester) or any of the leading West-country or Welsh clubs. After that season, however, the practice of one half acting as scrum-worker (or inside half) and the other standing off as outside half became fairly general, and practically every club adopts this formation now. I think the change has been for the good of the game, mainly because it has led to a better service from the scrum, whereby the threequarters have had the ball much more quickly than they used to, and so have greatly developed open play. The old style had its good points. I must say that I liked playing at outside half now and then: it was a change from the much more tiring work close in. Again, it tended to develop one's versatility, rather than having to specialise in one phase of play. Still, as I have said, the change is decidedly to the game's advantage. As the two halves, then, play a different game, we will take their individual play first.

THE INSIDE (OR SCRUM) HALF

There have been cases of big men making good scrum halves: W. I. Cheesman (O.M.T.'s and England), B. S. Cumberlege

(Cambridge – for England he played full back), and A. Hall (Gloucestershire – though latterly he has played forward) are cases in point. But, generally speaking, short, strong, and exceedingly agile men do best at scrum half. If you take your mind back over the past fifteen years of British Rugby, you will find that at least three-fourths of the inside halves have been men of this kind. This is mainly because the prime requisites of an inside half are nimbleness of foot and an ability to turn and twist quickly in a short space, both of which qualities are likely to be found in a small man than a big one. Now let us look at some of the duties of this player.

First, he has to put the ball into the scrummage – not an easy job at all. Forwards will, in their keenness, get their feet up, or the scrum will be pushed round, or the packing will be bad – all of which make it impossible to put the ball in properly. (Meanwhile, the crowd is yelling "Put the ball in!" or "What are you waiting for?") At last you see your chance, and in it goes, fairly fast and quite straight. Before this is done, however, the half should certainly shout out which side the ball is coming in "Coming left!" or "Coming right!" so that his forwards shall know where to expect it. Again, before the ball is put in, the half should know exactly what is going to happen should the ball come out his side. He should have arranged with his partner in which direction the back play is to be developed, *i.e.* to the right or to the left, or he should have arranged with the pack-leader if it is intended to keep the ball in and wheel. It is highly detrimental to the play of your side if you have ignored these precautions, for you will have precious little time to look for your partner when the ball does come out.

THE ART OF "FEEDING"

Let us suppose, first of all, that you have decided to feed

your backs if you get possession, and that the ball does come out your side. As soon as you see that your "hookers" have been successful, you must double round to the rear of your scrum as quickly as possible. A half who is slow in getting round jeopardises the chances of his backs tremendously. If he is slow, the time he takes enables his vis-a-vis or a "wing" forward to get on top of him and so perhaps to prevent him from passing at all, in addition to which it gives the whole of the opposing back division valuable time in which to adjust their mentality and (slightly) their position to defensive work rather than offensive. So an inside half should constantly be practising starts, and he can never be too quick off the mark for this purpose. Having reached the ball, he must be prepared to pick it up and throw out a swift hip-high pass in one movement, and in the necessary direction. This is a tall order, but this faculty for feeding the backs well is one of the hall-marks of a class inside half.

Like all things in sport, proficiency at this only comes by practice. I must have spent dozens of hours learning to dash at full speed to a stationary or very "slowly-moving" ball, pick it up, and "feed" my partner with a "true" pass. The system I had with my partner for many years (J. Stephens, Gloucester) was as follows: – I would stand over the ball (the ball being on the ground), and Stephens would be about five yards behind me. He would shout out which side he was coming – right or left just before he started, and I would scoop the ball to him straight from the ground, judging my pass to get into such a position as to enable him to take it with ease whilst going at full speed. This would be varied by my running to the ball, as though it had just come out of the scrum and I had dashed round to pass it out. The following diagrams will show what I mean.

As a result of continual practice I got to be able to "find" him nearly every time without looking for him. I could gauge where he would be in his run, and would throw the

ball about a foot in front of that spot, and rarely would we fail to connect.

Now a scrum half must be able to "find" the man he is passing to, in one of two ways. First, there is the "direct" pass. Here the body is slightly turned towards the receiver of the pass, and the half pushes the ball away, as it were, with both hands. It is most easily done, naturally, when the passer actually faces the direction in which the ball is to go. It is the normal way in which one man would pass a Rugby ball to another man. But circumstances, or tactics, often compel a half to give out another kind of pass – what is generally called the "reverse" pass. In this case the body is turned wholly or partly from the receiver of the pass, and the ball is thrown, not away from the front of the body, but back under one of the arms, and past the side of the body. This "reverse" pass is much more often used than the direct pass by the first class player. If the half is waiting at the base of the scrum for the ball to come out, he will have his back to his partner, and will gain time if he can get the ball away under one arm with a reverse pass. Again, if he dashes round to find the ball out waiting for him he will have to give a reverse pass, unless his partner is going in the same direction as himself, when a direct pass will be necessary.

A scrum half, then, must practise these two kinds of passes continually. At first it will seem hopeless; he will lack direction and speed in his passes, and he will require two movements – one in which to pick the ball up, and one in which to pass it. But by dint of persistence, surprising dexterity can be attained. Let him get a partner, his outside half for preference, and do what Stephens and I did, and he will soon improve. At first he may have to confine himself to looking at the man to whom he is going to pass; practice, however, will soon give him the ability to find his man without actually seeing him. It is far better to practise by daylight on the playing pitch, but splendid practice can be obtained in any hall or gymnasium. Many an hour did my partner and I spend "working up these connections" in the capital gymnasium on the Kingsholm (Gloucester) ground.

There are three other ways of getting the ball away. None of the three should be looked upon as normal, but they must all be practised, for I have seen them used, and have used them all myself, as the rare circumstances in which they are helpful have cropped up. First there is the "reverse" pass between the legs. A "fluke" I have heard it called frequently, but it can be done intentionally and well. An inside half may find himself well over the ball, and may get a peep of his partner between his legs, at the very second that he feels that his opponent is on top of him, in which case it is certainly advisable to throw out the pass that way. I remember one instance in particular, at Northampton, when I was playing for Plymouth. I found myself so placed that this sort of pass was the only possible one. My legs were rather wide apart, and I felt instinctively that the ball must go through my legs if my partner was to get it in time. Through my legs it went, and the outside half was clear in a flash. Some of the spectators near by cheered, some jeered, the latter probably thinking it was either a case of sheer luck or of playing to the gallery. As I said, I don't advise any inside half to set out to try this shot of ten – above all, with a view to appealing to the "gallery" (which tendency he will find it difficult to check if he once yields to it); but I should advise him to be prepared to use it as occasion demands. I have seen some halves, succumbing to the "call" of the gallery, send out swift "between-the-legs" passes that have enabled their opponents to score, for the ball has gone very wide of the mark, to give an opponent a clear run in-hard lines on the passer's side, but a fate that "playing to the gallery" deserves.

Then R. A. Jago, the old Devon and England "scrum" half, was particularly adept at passing from the ground with one hand only. Often have I been on top of him when the ball was out, only to see him lean well forward and "push" a good pass with one hand to J. Peters, his partner. It takes a lot of doing, and I don't recommend any scrum half to practise it much – I could never do it myself with any satisfaction, though I tried it in training. But there it is: I have seen it used to great advantage, and if any scrum half finds he can do it easily, he had better keep the idea by him for occasional use.

The other way is also a dangerous one, but a man who has played a lot of Association may find himself able to do it. I mean passing the ball out with your foot. Very rarely is it any advantage to use this method of passing, even though the half can do it, but there are times when you may find yourself so placed as to make this the best way. I should advise a scrum half to practise it a little, but to use it rarely. I must emphasise the fact that two-handed direct passes are the basis of all service from the scrum, and the scrum half must practise assiduously, so as to be able to give these in one motion when the ball is on the ground. When he can do this he should learn to give the reverse pass-a fascinating shot, and well worth a lot of practice. Not until he can pass in both these ways can he ever hope to be a good "feeder" an important aspect of a scrum half's play.

THE REVERSE PASS

I should like to say a word or two more about the reverse pass before we leave the subject of passing from the base of the scrum. As I have said above, in essence, a reverse pass is one that is given in the opposite direction to that in which the half is facing or running, and the ball is generally thrown under one arm. It will be found that, in addition to other advantages, continual practice will enable a man to throw the ball with greater force this way than by the direct method. One seems to be able to get more "push" from the wrists and forearm in this way. From 1906 to 1914 there was far more use made of the reverse pass than there has been since 1919. In fact, so rarely have I seen it used in all the games I have seen since 1919, that I consider it an "event" to see it. There can be no reason except that halves don't practise it, for they get the same opportunities of using it as the pre-War players, unless it be that the War and the flux of time have removed the past-masters of the art, and the learners of to-day have never seen it done properly a sad fact that applies, I am afraid, to many phases of the game. R. M. Owen, the Welsh scrum-half for many years, and easily the cleverest "feeder" I have ever seen or played against, improved upon the normal reverse pass in a brilliant fashion. Instead of passing straight from the ground, he would, when in possession of the ball, at times make off towards the right, for example. By arrangement, his threequarters on that side of the field would make off in the same direction, which, of course, meant that their opponents made for the same part of the field. After going a few yards, he would, whilst still going hard to the right, send a magnificent reverse pass to his partner or a centre who had stood back on the left, and the receiver of the pass and another player, a wing threequarter generally, would be left practically clear to make ground on that side.

This was the stratagem that enabled Wales to beat New Zealand (the "All Blacks") at Cardiff Arms Park in 1906, the only defeat the Colonials sustained. It was Owen who conceived the idea, I believe, and I have often seen him use it in club matches.

Only a set of threequarters that was absolutely *en rapport* with a pair of halves who knew each other's play inside out could try this manoeuvre with any chance of success; and for the Wales *v.* New Zealand match it was rehearsed off the field first of all, and then on the field the day before the match. The scrum was formed about fifteen yards from the New Zealanders' goal-line and about the same distance from the touch-line. Owen made off with the ball towards the open field, took the opposition with him, gave the reverse pass to P. F. Bush, who sent E. T. Morgan over in the corner.

The idea was copied by some clever club halves, especially T. H. Vile and W. J. Martin, but I haven't seen it tried for years. I commend it to any pair of halves who are likely to play together for any length of time, and who can get a couple of threequarters to work with them. It is advanced Rugby, I know, but there is tremendous pleasure in bringing the trick off. So much, then, for service from the base of the scrummage.

GOING ON ONE'S OWN

One of the great dangers of specialising at scrum half is that players are apt to think that when their side gets possession they must pass the ball out; in other words, they must never go on their own. Mind, of the two evils of a scrum half going on his own too often and passing out too often, the former is much the greater. The good player realises that to serve his backs is his main function, but he also realises that he can best do this by going on his own now and then, so as to keep his opponents guessing as to whether he is coming through by himself, or whether the backs are going to get the ball. It is decidedly disconcerting to a back division to be ready to tackle their opponents, man for man, in a threequarter movement, only to find a determined dash made by the scrum half right through the middle of them. In this respect, no scrum half that I have seen has equalled C. A. Kershaw (Royal Navy and England). It has been a most exhilarating sight to see this sturdy half ignoring his partner, and dashing up midfield with the pace and skill of a centre and the determination of a forward. In the England *v*. Ireland match at Dublin in 1922 England won by four tries to one, and of the four that England scored, three were entirely due to breaks-away by Kershaw, in which he ran through the middle of his opponents, and finally passed to a colleague who had simply to run in unopposed.

When to go on one's own is a matter to be decided generally by the inside half himself. He can see whether the opposition are beginning to anticipate his pass and to close up on his backs, ignoring the possibility that he will go on his own. When he sees this happening, he must realise that his chance has come. He must give a sharp glance at the disposition of the opposing backs, and especially the opposing halves, so as to see which will be the better direction. As a rule, it is better for the half to run towards the side further from the referee (assuming, of course, that the ball was put in on the referee's side), for then, if the opportunity is a perfect one, he will be able to dash round the scrum, pick up the ball on the run, and cut up the field without any loss of time. Many a match has been won by a brainy scrum half after a dash of this kind from a scrum close to his opponents' line. Incidentally, I ought to say here that when these dashes are made, the outside half should, as a rule, participate in the manoeuvre, if only by acting as a "blind"; but what the precise function of that player is under these circumstances, I will leave till later. There will be occasions, however, on which a scrum half can deceive even his partner, when he is satisfied that an ideal opportunity has presented itself. The backs will start as though a passing movement is about to take place, and the outside half will maneuver as though he is going to get the ball. It is only a very watchful opposition indeed that can stop a scrum half who chooses the psychological moment to deceive not only his opponents but his own colleagues.

On very wet grounds, it is advisable to refrain from picking up the ball as a rule, even though it comes out on your side, by far the better plan being to go off with a dribble. Obviously, it is difficult to pick up a greasy ball on a muddy ground, and then to pass it with any accuracy. A scrum half should, for this reason, put in plenty of practice at dribbling, especially on wet grounds. The man who can control the ball with his feet under these conditions will have plenty of chances of clearing his side out of tight corners, and of getting them into better positions to attack; whilst many a try has been scored by a nippy half, following a direct dribble from a scrummage ten or fifteen yards from his opponents' line. I should like to emphasise this aspect of a scrum half's play, for it is often neglected. It is tantalising to see a good team let down because a keen but thoughtless scrum half will persist in trying to pick up a wet ball instead of using his feet to it. Every back ought to participate in dribbling practice. If a man has played Association, he will find it very useful. I know I found the six years of Association I played before taking to Rugby most helpful to me.

RUSH-STOPPING

The scrum half will often have to perform what is always looked upon as a thankless task, *viz*. rush-stopping. When A. Tedford (Ireland) – one of the finest forwards at a rush and close dribble that I have ever seen – and three or four other Irish forwards came dashing up the field with the ball admirably under control, one needed more than a little pluck to go down to check their progress, and it is generally the scrum half who has to do this, for most of these rushes start from the scrummage or lines-out, when the scrum half is the first of the backs to be encountered. But always assuming that the "rushers" will play the game, which means in this case that they will kick at the ball and not at the man who stops the rush, there is a fascination in stopping rushes. Certainly pluck is the prime requisite in the rush-stopper, though skill is also necessary.

This was the principle on which I always worked. With the best dribbler in the world (that is, of a Rugby ball) there is always a fraction of a second in about every five yards when the ball is not absolutely under control. If you watch, you can see that moment, and that is the time to dash across the front of the dribbler, take the ball from his feet, and either to run diagonally up the field, or else give a short punt into touch or over the heads of the rushing forwards. You may have to go back a few yards with the oncoming forwards before you see your chance; but it will come, and with practice you will get remarkably adept at spotting your chance. Great agility is required on the part of the man who goes down to a rush in this way, for if he is a wee bit too soon or too late in his dash, he is asking for, and will assuredly get, trouble. But I have seen this method pay time and time again, and I commend it as the foundation of successful rush-stopping, a glorious phase of Rugby in

A FORWARD RUSH

that it calls for any amount of pluck and not a little skill, an ideal combination of qualities.

If the rush, however, is near your own line, you cannot afford to give ground in this way, and the other method must be adopted. Here the rush stopper hurls himself at the ball more directly towards the dribbler, so that he will fall, with the ball in his possession, against the dribbler's shin or instep, neither of which can hurt him very much. Injuries happen when the man drops on the ball just as the dribbler is taking his next kick, and the former falls away from the dribbler, as it were, so as to be in a position to receive the toe of the dribbler. That way lies serious trouble, and it is not always the dribbler's fault.

Another cause of injuries in rush-stopping is entirely due to the man who falls on the ball, because of his refusal to play the ball after stopping the rush. The rule says that the man in possession and on the ground must either let the ball go free or play it with his feet. If he curls himself round it, with the best of intentions from his side's point of view, he stands a capital chance of getting badly kicked by an exasperated forward. In addition, he should be instantly penalised, for justice must be done to the dribbler as well as the "stopper," for all the latter's pluck. Nothing appeals to the sporting instinct of the onlooker so much as rush-stopping. Consequently, in a game where pluck is one of the greatest qualities developed, rush-stopping should be practised, and the best rush-stopper in the side should be the scrum half.

Pluck and agility, then, are qualities that a scrum half must possess. In addition, he must be able to "feed" well, to go on his own judiciously, to dribble properly, and to stop rushes. There are many other things that he will find useful; but if he can do these properly, he will not be a bad player! I played in that position for a dozen years, and for all the buffeting I got, if I had my playing days over again

I should take up the same position, so attractive did I find the play there.

4
Half-Back Play (Part Two)

THE OUTSIDE HALF

The outside half is often referred to as the pivot of the side, and it is a fitting term to apply to him, for upon him practically the whole of the machinery of the side hinges. The strongest threequarter line is rendered well-nigh powerless by a weak outside half; whilst what is generally looked upon as a weak line can be almost forced to do splendid work if they have in front of them a brilliant outside half. Physically, the ideal man for the position is the medium-sized man, something around five feet eight in height, and between ten and eleven stone in weight. The best outside halves I have ever seen have possessed this kind of physique. In addition, they should be very quick off the mark, able to take the most awkward of passes and to give good ones, able to kick with either foot, be possessed of plenty of pluck, and, above all, have an eye for an opening.

Now many of these qualities can be developed to a great degree by practice. Quickness off the mark is essentially an art to be acquired in training, not during the game itself. The same thing applies to the ability to kick with either foot. This needs a deal of practice, and, to be candid, very rarely does any player acquire equal dexterity with either foot. But for a man to be a splendid kick with the right foot and a hopeless one with the left is strongly to be condemned. By all means, keep developing any natural ability with one foot; but an outside half should work hard, though it will go against the grain, to be comparatively useful with the other foot. Naturally, when he can, he will use his "better" foot, but he will frequently find himself so placed when to kick with that foot would be to let his side down.

There is a special sort of kicking that the outside half should try to become proficient at, and that is the short punt, given with good direction and strength up to distances of about forty yards. Later on in this section, the usefulness of this will be explained. Two or three players can soon develop this art. Let one have five minutes with the ball, whilst the others stand the necessary distances away, and about ten yards apart. Then the kicker should try to drop the ball with a short punt into the hands of each of his partners in turn. The various players in turn can take the kicker's place. When proficiency at one distance has been acquired, the distance can be increased; but there is no need to do this intensive practice at distances of more than about forty yards, for a punt longer than that will rarely be needed for the purpose I have in mind. When this short punt can be done reasonably well with the better foot, it must be practised with the other foot, and what duffers most players will find themselves at it to begin with! The next stage is to practise the same thing on the run, and it can be done, of course, by taking short runs at increasing speeds before punting. The outside half who can do this short punt well will win many a match for his side. It is another manoeuvre one rarely sees done well nowadays, although, to my mind, it is one of the normal means an outside half should use for penetrating his opponents' defence.

DROP-KICKING

Again, the outside half should practise drop kicking, for

he is certain to get plenty of chances of dropping at goal during a game, though woe betide him if he tries too often and misses! Who that has seen them will ever forget some of W. J. A. Davies's dropped goals, the one for the Royal Navy against the Army in 1922, to name but one of many? Or take P. F. Bush, the old Welsh International, who was also a clever drop-kicker. Both these men were marvels at the "snap" drop for goal; in fact they were probably geniuses, for I cannot imagine a lifetime spent at practising, enabling a player to become a Davies or a Bush, without that spark of genius that these two added to mechanical ability. Still, amazing improvement can be achieved by practicing quick shots at goal from a radius of about twenty-five yards from the posts. Try them directly from the front, then from the sides, now standing still to take the shot, now on the run, now with a sharp turn round at the last second, and so on. Ring the changes on these ideas, always having in mind the ideal of being able to kick a goal from this distance on the run, with a momentary glance at the posts, and after a quick decision to make the attempt.

A SAFE PAIR OF HANDS

The stand-off half who hasn't hands like a good fielder in the slips had better change his position, for he is comparatively useless if he cannot take all sorts and conditions of passes, and, in nearly every case, whilst well under way. This faculty can be acquired by steady practice on the lines detailed in the previous chapter. At first, of course, he should be able to take only normal passes, *i.e.* passes hip high, and well in front of him, whilst he is going at a steady pace. Next he should quicken his pace, and be prepared to pull in any pass that is not actually behind him! This seems like a counsel of perfection; but really it is not, for men like

W. J. A. Davies, A. D. Stoop, "Pat" Munro, H. Coverdale, M. Magee, R. Jones, and J. Stephens used to pull in passes that it was apparently impossible for any human being to hold. I know I have sent my various partners passes I was very much ashamed of, but they have fetched them in somehow and the pass has then been pronounced a splendid one! The "splendidness" lay in the taking, not in the giving. One thing I always endeavoured to do, and that was to get the ball in front of the outside half. With that precaution, I knew that my partner might take the pass. If the ball drops behind the poor outside half, he is helpless, needless to say. High above the head, right down at the instep, wide on the left or right, as fast as a shot out of a gun, all must be taken and held at the first attempt. If an outside half can do that, he is armed with the principal weapon a player in his position can possess.

The complement of this, of course, is that he should be able to part with the ball so that the other fellow can take it. And here his very virtue becomes a vice all too often. Many a player who takes his passes superbly, expects other players to be equally adept, and throws them really bad passes, through sheer carelessness. It should be every passer's endeavour to give the receiver the best pass possible under the circumstances, thus ensuring the probability that it will be take cleanly and without loss of time. I have seen outside halves, after brilliant work, throw the ball away in the most haphazard manner, often without looking at the intended receiver, and yards out of his reach, with the result that their previous good play has been quite spoilt by the splendid opening given to their opponents when the ball has fallen yards away from their own colleagues. The outside half, then, should try to be equally adept at giving and taking a pass, for so much depends upon accuracy in these respects.

PENETRATING THE DEFENCE

The other quality mentioned at the beginning of this section, *viz*. having an eye for an opening, is much more difficult to write about, for this gift cannot be acquired by mechanical practice, but only comes by plenty of match play, and then only to the man who has the Rugby "head" to size up the disposition of his opponents, and see at a glance the weak point in their defence. Now the ways by which an outside half can help his side to penetrate his opponents' defence are many; but these are the chief: –

1. By starting a bout of swift, mechanical passing.
2. By going through on his own after a feint, or by means of a cut through; and
3. By means of a short punt.

In the first case, the outside half's duty is to take his pass when well on the run, to see that he draws the opponent he has marked out for that purpose, and to time his pass so that the receiver is not tackled as soon as he gets the ball, but has it in time to do something with it. A danger the outside half will have to guard against is the tendency to run across the field, at right angles to the touch-line. Obviously it will be impossible, and inadvisable if it were possible, to start a successful passing bout of this kind by running straight up the field, for the defence would close in on him and his "threes" and soon check the movement. The ideal angle at which to run is one about 45° with the line joining the centre of the scrum, with the outside half when standing behind waiting for the ball. Again, he must not delay his pass, for the longer he holds the ball, the more will his opponents be able to align themselves so as to mark the right men.

In the second case, the point to remember is that the endeavour of the outside half is to get behind one or more of the opposing backs before parting with the ball, and, in some cases, where he is brilliantly successful, say from near the line, he will not need to part with the ball, but will score on his own. If he can get behind the defence, his opponents will find it hard to catch him, for he will be well under way going in one direction, whilst they will be behind him going in the other direction. Take the feint first: the outside half has to convince his immediate opponent or opponents that he is going to pass, so that they leave him and make for the man to whom they think he is going to pass. This, of course, is also known as "selling the dummy." To do it properly, a man must deceive his opponents in every way possible. He should look as though it is a dead certainty that he is going to pass. It should be writ large on his face by his glancing towards the would-be receiver, he should sway his body in the same direction when about to make the feint, and at the right moment he should take the ball back slightly as though actually on the point of sending it on its journey. Some go so far as to send the ball across the body, say from the left to the right, checking it with the right arm when apparently it was leaving the body; but the cleverest "feinters" do not do this. (I have referred to W. Spiers and H. L. Price as a couple of players who have done this well.) The body sway, the facial expression, and the arm action are enough. Then as soon as the outside half has made the feint, and sees that the fellow who has "bought the dummy" has started on his false errand, the former should increase his speed as much as possible, especially for the first few yards, so as to get clear of any arms stretched out when the trick has been noticed. The idea of the feint is to get the man or men who should be coming for you to go for somebody else, and thus enable you to get behind them. The trick takes a lot of doing, and the timing of it needs long practice before the ability to do it at the best possible moment is acquired.

The "cut-through" is a different manoeuvre. Generally it is done by a sharp change of direction when on the run, sometimes with, and sometimes without, the assistance of the feint. Let us suppose that your outside half is opening out the game towards his right. He makes off as though he is going to start the normal bout of passing referred to in method one. The opposition bears across that way to check it. When he sees his opponents well under way towards that quarter, he suddenly changes his direction by a sharp push-off on the right foot, and instead of going up the field in an oblique direction, makes off in a line almost parallel to the touch-line, the change of direction enabling him to get behind the men he would have run into had he gone straight on. It requires a lot of skill to do this well, but it can be practised a lot in training, by learning to change direction when on the run. When this has been mastered, the next thing is to learn when the opposition is so placed as to make it possible to do it, and this comes only after match practice – and not then, if the player does not possess the "eye for an opening" referred to above. The feint and "cut through" are generally worked together, though, as will be seen from what I have said, the latter can be done quite effectively without a feint. The side-step is another way by which the outside half can go through "on his own."

Then there is the short punt, the best method against a very strong defence. Sometimes, if your side is getting the ball out from nearly every scrum, your opponents line up level with the scrum (and in front of it, if the referee is not wide-awake!), and so give you less room to work in than you like. As soon as the ball comes out, they rush up to your men and often are on top of them simultaneously with their receiving the ball, so that the attack is nipped in the bud. Those are the conditions under which the short punt should be used. The stand-off half should give the tip to his threequarters that he is going to punt, and then as soon as he sees the defence coming down hard towards the threequarters he should give a short punt over the opposing threequarters' heads, towards a part of the field furthest from the full-back, and his threequarters ought to be able to do something with the opening thus given them. Many a try has followed these tactics, but even when a try has not followed, the tactics have caused the defence to keep further back, thus giving your more room to work in. The great difficulty in carrying out this short punt is that the Rugby ball is a law unto itself in the matter of bouncing. A perfect punt may be ruined by the ball bouncing badly. No precaution can dispense with that danger – even a Davies cannot ensure a bounce that will be "takeable" on the run. That is one of the many glorious uncertainties in Rugby. All the man who is nearest the ball can do is to watch the ball very carefully so as to see, as far as he can, what it is going to do, before he makes the attempt to field it.

DROPPING FOR GOAL

The drop-kick as a means of attack has been referred to previously. It must not be used unless other means of penetrating your opponent's defence have failed. An outside half must never get it into his head that if he gets possession within reasonable distance of the goal-posts he is to have a shot for goal, for even if he is successful a time or two and wins the game for his side, it is not in the true spirit of Rugby to keep "potting" for goal. I contend that his prime duty is to play to his backs, and that his main endeavour should be to try to penetrate the defence in conjunction with his colleagues. If this fails, then he might have a drop for goal. Let us look at it another way. What would happen if it were accepted that it is sound Rugby for the half-back to drop for goal whenever possible? Every time there was a scrum within forty yards of the goal, the threequarters of the side who obtained possession could put their hands into their pockets whilst the outside half, quickly fed by the scrum half, had a shot for goal! What is more, this practice makes for selfishness. The drop for goal, then, should be used sparingly, and only when all other methods of winning a match seem unavailing. Many have thought so strongly on this that they have long advocated a reduction of the value of a dropped goal to two points, on the principle that it is not equivalent to a try; and there is a lot to be said for the idea. I cannot go so far as these people, however, and think that with the right spirit animating a side, which implies only an occasional use made of the drop for goal, there is no need to tamper with rules that, however illogical many of them seem to be, have in the mass made the game what it is. If the outside half does decide to drop for goal, he should stand deeper than usual (this will give him a little more time), and when he gets possession, either at once from a stationary position, or after going a stride or two, he should put in his kick. This may be varied by a sudden change of direction, *e.g.* a few strides towards the left, a sharp turn on the heel, and a quick shot at goal with the right foot. I shall always look upon W. J. A. Davies's dropped goal in the Army *v.* Navy match of 1922 as my *locus classicus* for dropped goals. From a loose scrum he darted to the left, cut in to the right, swerved past an opponent or two, and from a spot about thirty yards from the goal-line and about twenty yards to the left of the left-hand post, sent the ball over the cross-bar with a perfect left-foot kick. The next best shot I have seen was the one kicked by W. J. Wallace, the New Zealander. It was in the last match of their famous tour, against Swansea at Swansea. The latter were deservedly leading by a try scored by W. J. Scrines, when Wallace dropped a beautiful goal, though partly tackled, and from quite sixty yards, a strong wind helping the ball along. The

All Blacks won by this dropped goal to Swansea's try.

On the defence, an outside half should be able to tackle well, though I must confess that the most brilliant players in this position have more often than not been poor tacklers, and their defensive work has lain chiefly in judicious kicking. Still, no outside half can consider himself a really capable player if he despises the art of tackling, and I advise all youngsters taking the game up to learn it. After all, why should any player leave to someone else the task of checking his opponents in a manner that demands pluck above everything else? "I don't mind if he doesn't tackle a man all the afternoon. All I want him for is his attack," I have heard captains say sometimes. This presupposes that there are other willing backs prepared to shoulder the half's burdens on the defence, which may or may not be good for the side. At all events, if it can be said of any man, "He can't tackle," it detracts from his merits as a footballer at once. So I say that an outside half should be able to do his part in the defence by tackling, kicking, and rush-stopping, though I admit that he should be strongest in kicking.

5

Half-Back Play (Part Three)

THE HALVES IN COMBINATION

In discussing the play of the half-backs as separate entities, continual reference has been made to their play in relation to one another. Two half-backs must always understand that however brilliant they might be individually, their positions demand that they must, by dint of hard practice, learn to dovetail into one another's movements, and they must also learn to develop their tactics so that any good work they do will lead up to opportunities for the rest of the side, generally the threequarters, to crown what they have commenced. A selfish half-back, be he an inside or an outside, will ruin the play of any team. It really is very fascinating (*experto crede*) for a pair of halves to work together and try to develop a complete understanding with one another. To do this properly, any amount of practice is needed off the field, on the lines detailed in the early part of Chapter 3, and, in addition, the utmost watchfulness is necessary whilst the game is in progress. Each will gradually get to know, without any signs being given, what the other will do under certain circumstances, and the most watchful opposition is outwitted by the manoeuvring of a pair of halves absolutely *en rapport*. It is well to start, however, with some code of signals, especially at the scrummage, so that the inside half shall know to which side of the field his partner is going to run if the ball comes out his side. And here let me interpose a strong protest against calling this "shady tactics." For many years it was almost the custom to look upon anything particularly clever, especially where the collusion of a few players was necessary, as decidedly "shady." The game of Rugby, by excellent and well-meaning folk, was regarded as a glorious game for the physically very fit, where strength was the main requisite; and if a side that played that kind of football – honest, manly, and vigorous all of it – was beaten by a side that executed a few well-conceived manoeuvres cleverly, there was a pronounced tendency to dub the winners as a "shady" lot. Fortunately that practice has almost disappeared, but it is to be found occasionally, hence this protest.

Many little tricks have been devised by various pairs of halves for the purpose of signalling to each other. The commonest is for the outside half to tap the outside of his thigh on the side in which he proposes to run, *e.g.* if he intends going to the right he will tap the outside of his right thigh with the right hand. Needless to say, this should be done as surreptitiously as possible, for the other fellows, if they are doing their work properly, should be looking out for these signals. Still, it is surprising how frequently your opponents are not aware of your intentions, simply because they are engaged in the same operation at the same time! With great care, this "tapping the leg" signal meets the requirements and forms a satisfactory *modus operandi*. The great thing is to do it as carefully as possible, watching the other side so that you can pass the signal when they are not looking at you. The outside-half should not decide which way he is going until he sees the disposition of the other backs, and this will be when the scrum is practically formed. Then the scrum half is at the opening of the scrum, either waiting to put the ball in, or close against his *vis-á-vis* who is going to put it in. Immediately before the ball is put in, if the signal has not been given before, the scrum half should turn his head sharply and look for the signal. Having obtained that, he will know exactly where his partner will be when the ball comes out, and he can set him going properly. I have seen a pair of halves work this signal neatly by means of a wink – not too easily seen by the opposing outside half! Others I have seen give a gentle nod of the head.

A plan my partner and I in the Gloucestershire team found very successful was as follows: – The referee always stands on one side of the scrummage when the ball is put in. Well, the side he was on we called "Yes"; the other side "No." This dispensed with the terms "Open" and "Short." We generally managed to find an opportunity of passing this word to each other without the other side hearing, and for a long time it nonplussed most of our opponents even if they did hear it, for they did not understand it. At last, however, other halves copied the idea, and we had to be doubly careful to get the word passed in a whisper. It is the scrum half who benefits most by a signal of this kind, for, if he knows exactly which way his partner is going, he can often mislead his opponents by going one way himself, and so starting his opponents on a false scent, and then throwing a reverse pass to his partner, who will know that the first dash was only a ruse, and will ignore it, to the extent of going off in the opposite direction, knowing full well that the ball will eventually come in the prearranged direction. Touring teams often have an advantage, for if they speak another language, they often use a word or phrase that is unintelligible to us. Welsh clubs find this idea useful, and many and many a splendid English, Scottish, or Irish side has been beaten by a subtle use of the Welsh language. The backs would conform to a certain alignment, that had all the appearance of a particular kind of attack, and the non-Welsh side would prepare to check it. The feint would be made in that direction, but the actual attack would be

INTERCEPTING A PASS

delivered elsewhere, thanks to a word or phrase delivered in Welsh at the last minute. I know a little Welsh myself, and have found it useful more than once. I remember one great game at Gloucester when we were playing Swansea, then at the height of their fame. Try as they would they could not penetrate our defence, but just towards the end of the game they made one superb effort. They forced us to our own "25" and had a scrum about twenty yards from our line, and about the same distance from the touch-line. As usual, they obtained possession, but they kept it in the back row, and continued to push our pack steadily towards our line, the ball being admirably controlled by Ivor Morgan, who was playing in the back row. Then, with much ostentation, they all aligned to attack towards the open field, and off our men went. But I had heard R. M. Owen shout in Welsh to George Davies (one of his centres) that he was coming to the short side. So I slipped around the scrum quickly, and managed to intercept the pass that Owen sent to Davies, when the latter was practically clear. But even a knowledge of Welsh is rarely sufficient to check a skilful Welsh side, and seeing that these attacks were not likely to get home, they proceeded to beat "from afar" – Davies dropping a goal just on time. The halves, then, must have some code, and the few I have mentioned are some I have seen or used myself, and have found quite easy to work.

Again, the half-backs must combine in some prearranged way for the purpose of defence, if the ball comes out the other side. There are two ideas in practice. Let us call "A" and "A1" the scrum half and outside half respectively of one side, and "B" and "B1" the same players on the other side, and assume that the ball is coming out on "B's" side of the scrum. One method is for "A" to follow the ball as it is being heeled, and when he thinks "B" is just about to pass, to dash after "B1," ignoring "B" for the time. This often enables "A" to tackle "B1" before the latter has got into his stride. Suppose "B" does not pass to "B1," however, but sees "A's" game, and goes through on his own, after a feint that sets "A" going on his fruitless journey. Well, "A1" will see to him – that is "A1's" duty. He is to watch from the back of the scrum, to see whether "B" is coming on his own: if he is, of course, he should be able to tackle him, because he is admirably placed for that purpose. On the other hand, if "B" does pass, then "A1" makes off for "B1," or the player who is nearest "B1," and is likely to receive the pass from "B1." I remember a pair of halves who brought this method to a fine art, and it needed a very clever pair to open an attack against them.

The other method, and by far the commoner, is for each half to take his *vis-á-vis*, *i.e.* "A" will take "B," and "A1" "B1." "A" will follow the ball to the back of the scrum, keeping behind it all the time, needless to say, and then endeavour to pounce upon "B," just as the latter is about to pass the ball or make off with it. What is more, "A" must not be content to tackle "B" round the hips or waist, for that will not prevent "B" from passing the ball. The tackle must have the effect of making "B" quite unable to part with the ball, so that "A" must endeavour to lock "B's" arms to his side with the tackle, or if he is unable to do that, to catch hold of one of "B's" arms, and so render "B" incapable of using that arm to pass with. Again, if "B" is slow at picking up the ball, "A" may be able to pick it up for him! (I have seen this done more than once, when a nippy scrum half has been opposed to one on the slow side.) Or he may be able, perhaps, to dribble it away, just as "B" is going to pick it up. In this method, then, one scrum half devotes all his attention to the other scrum half , and tries to nip the movement in the bud, *i.e.* at the base of the scrum. Meanwhile, the outside half, "A1," is watching. He must not start off until there is more than a probability that the backs are going to get the ball at once, for if the opposing scrum half, "B," should elude "A," it will be "A1's" task to stop him.

These are the two commonest modes of checking the opposing halves when the latter are in possession. Personally I found the second the better method to use as a general principle, though my various partners and I have had occasional resort to the former, just to vary our tactics. I will say this, however, that I have never seen defensive work immediately outside the scrummage done so effectively as by the two half-backs referred to above. Both were absolutely fair, and tackled one or the other of the opposing halves, in possession, seven times out of ten. The way to make this method less effective, of course, was for the outside half to stand very deep, but even that had its drawbacks, for it gave the scrum half, "A," a better chance of intercepting the pass from "B" to "B1," and if "A" had the sense of anticipation well developed, the pass *was* intercepted.

As regards throwing out of touch, it is recognised that the scrum half should always throw out of touch, thus enabling the outside half to take up a position where he is likely to be most useful if the ball should happen to be passed back by a forward. This position is, as a rule, about three or four yards nearer his own goal-line than the line-out is, and somewhere in the vicinity of the middle of the line, though this will be modified by circumstances. It is a good plan, though, for the outside half to throw out of line sometimes, especially when it has been decided to keep the ball to the forwards from the line-out. This gives the hardest-worked man on the field at all times, *viz.* the scrum half, a little rest, for continual throwing out of touch makes the shoulders very sore. If the other side throws in, the scrum half should stand close in, to stop any "short-line" tricks, whilst his partner should watch his opponents and conform to their disposition, so as to be best able to help in the defence. In general play, the halves must always be on the lookout

OUT OF TOUCH

for each other. The outside half should get as close as is necessary to the scrum half if the latter seems likely to get the ball from some loose play, and the latter on his part should always realise that when he gets the ball, the chances are that his alter ego is hovering about waiting to carry on the good work to the backs, and so the scrum half should always look round to see if his partner is conveniently situated to help him to open out the game.

The functions of both halves are in some respects really much about the same. The scrum half's chief work is to pass on, as cleverly as he can, to his partner the chances his forwards give him, varying it by going on his own; whilst the outside halfs' main object is to pass on as cleverly as he can the chances his scrum half gives him, varying it by going on his own.

Fortunate is the side that has a pair of halves each of whom knows his duties as an individual player and as part of a machine: that side will not go far wrong.

6

Threequarter Play (Part One)

THE THREEQUARTERS

Almost every club nowadays adopts the four-threequarter game, so I propose to confine myself almost entirely to a consideration of the play of a line of threequarters consisting of four players. The most important clubs that do not are Leicester and Bath, who regularly play five-threequarters. But all that follows applies with equal force to a five-threequarter line as to one with four-threequarters. Every member of the line must realise that he has two entities, as it were. He is part of a machine, and his play must generally be in combination with the other three players or the machine will get out of gear and prove comparatively useless. In addition, however, he must never forget that he has always to develop his own individual play. A slavish adherence to the "combination" idea ruins back play. It tends to make it mechanical and generally ineffective. On the other hand, too much individualism, especially in the centre, will never help a side to win a match.

As is generally the case, a compromise brings about the best results. The basis of all threequarter play must be the combination of the four players: each man must play in such a way as to enable the other members of the line to carry on effectively the good work he has done. This must be varied by the ability of the centres to go on their own, when they see that their opponents have arranged themselves to ward off a combined attack, so leaving a possible opening for an individual burst through.

Years ago, back play consisted of a series of individual dashes, and very exhilarating they must have been. Then it was found, however, that the attack was more effectively carried out if the members of the threequarter line sank a little of their individuality and generally conformed to the play of their fellows. Latterly, the pendulum has swung too far in this direction, and one sees the combination idea carried to excess. The prevailing thought to the back who receives the ball seems to be: to whom can I pass? The result is that you often find him, as soon as he gets possession, glancing around to see who shall get it next, instead of going on and doing his best to improve the position before parting with the ball. Threequarters must never forget these dual functions, *viz.* as individual players, and as parts of a machine. Many a time in recent years have I sighed for a return to the old days, as I have seen the ball going right along the threequarter line, with little or no ground gained, every player apparently thinking that it was his sole duty to take a pass and give one neatly.

The ideal line is one where both these kinds of play are mixed; as the result of plenty of practice together, each member of the line gets to know the idiosyncrasies of the others, and when one goes on his own, the others quickly back him up, knowing what he is likely to attempt under the circumstances. I don't think I have ever seen this mixture of individualism and combination better illustrated than in the Welsh team of 1902–05, when the threequarter line consisted of E. T. Morgan and W. M. Llewelyn on the wing and Gwyn Nicholls and R. T. Gabe in the centre. Both the centres were big men, and their favourite variation of the conventional passing movement was a strong dash through the opposing line of threequarters. The New Zealanders of 1905, the South Africans of 1906, and the Oxford team of

1909 were other sides that had superb backs who mixed these two kinds of play admirably. If a man contemplates playing in the threequarter line, then he must realise his dual functions or else give up the idea of playing there, especially if he is a centre.

Now let us take the centres first. For preference, a centre should be well made and full of pluck, for it is a position in which a player has a lot of hard work to do, and he will need not only skill for attacking purposes, but great grit for defensive purposes. The centre should learn to tackle well, to give and to take a pass when on the run, to kick well with one foot, if not with both, to go down to forward rushes, and to spot an opening almost before it shows itself! The outside half and the centres must know one another's play inside out, for that is the little triumvirate that regulates the whole of the back play of a side. If one of these fails, the whole team suffers. These three should try all sorts of tricks off the field, and work out plans that they propose trying under certain conditions. It is a splendid plan to get a box of matches and arrange your side on the table, and then set each other problems as to how a certain manoeuvre might be tried, and how it might be checked.

On the field, the centres should watch their halves as closely as possible. Every time a scrum is formed they should know which way the outside half intends going, to the right or to the left, so as to be ready to back him up. This information they should pass on to their wing for the same reason. If a centre is going to carry on a passing movement of a mechanical nature – that is, he is not going to attempt to go through on his own – his work is much the same as detailed for an outside half in the same connection. He must choose an opponent whom he is going to draw, and when he has drawn him, and he sees that his fellow-centre, or the wing, as the case might be, is well placed to receive the ball, he should pass the ball to him, a swift and true pass. If, on the other hand, a centre is going through on his own, he must either give the outside half the tip before the movement starts, so that the latter can adapt his play and give the centre the best opening he can, or he must pretend at the outset to be about to take part in a stereotyped passing bout before he goes on his own.

One thing a centre must most assiduously guard against, and that is running across the field. How often does one see the poor wing threequarter bored either close to or right into touch before getting possession, when, of course, it is almost useless for him to receive a pass. If a centre receives the ball after one or more players have run straight across the field, he must check the movement at once. He can do this by a sharp punt up the field towards the touch-line, or, better still, by making a dash through the defence by means of a cut-through or a feint – anything to stop the straight-across-the-field idea. Mind, this is not so easy as it looks. A player will find it exceedingly difficult to counteract the temptation, when the defence is well up and he seems to be covered by one or more opponents. But he must devise means of overcoming it, even though, to begin with, it results in his being tackled in pos session many times.

When a centre receives the ball from the outside half, he must start off by running as straight up the field as he possibly can; the more directly he is running towards the touch-line, the worse is his, play generally speaking. If the defence is so keen that he can't make much progress himself, he must decide in a flash whether the man next to him can do better. If he thinks so, he should pass at once to him, at the exact moment when the latter can do something with it.

On the other hand, should the next player be in at least as bad a position as the centre himself, and is not a *much* better player, the centre must either go through on his own, come what may, or try a short punt over the opponent's head. That is a principle that centres often overlook. They should hardly ever pass the ball to a man unless he is in a position to do more with it than they are, and if there is no man near them in that fortunate position, they must either go on their own, or give a short punt up the field, or kick to touch. Nothing is more irritating to a player than to receive a pass from a fellow when he – the former – is overwhelmed by the opposition.

Run as straight as you can, and see that the man to whom you are passing is well placed to do something with the ball, or don't pass it to him, but go on your own or kick: here is the essence of the functions of a centre as an attacking force.

A centre should be skilled, too, at intercepting; but it is a weapon dangerous to the user. When it succeeds it is wonderfully effective: when it fails, no curses are too loud or too deep for you! Still, the art of intercepting must be practised. The centre should train himself to watch the facial expressions of players, their arm actions and body swings, just before they are going to pass. Very careful watching will enable a man to know when his opponent is going to pass, and when this faculty has been highly developed, an occasional interception may be attempted. But it is a difficult art, for every player knows full well that the other man is only too anxious to "sell him the dummy," and will endeavour by facial expression, arm action, and body swing to convince him absolutely that he is going to pass. Still, even a realisation of this should not deter a centre from trying to intercept sometimes. He must consider, in addition to the visible signs of an impending pass, whether the man in possession is in the habit of letting the ball go nearly every time, or whether he is an adept at "selling the dummy." I have known fellows get very expert at intercepting, but my advice to any young player is: be very chary about using the interception. It is far better to go for the man with the ball every time, even though he does pass it just as you tackle him. Again, the man who is addicted to trying to intercept is generally looked upon as a bit of a "funk," who prefers this flashy mode of stopping an attack to the more prosaic and pluck-needing one of tackling the man in possession and it is often true! Still, the idea of intercepting must be borne in mind, though practised with great discretion.

A centre threequarter needs to be fairly fast: slow-moving men in the middle of the threequarter line can practically never give wings the chances they require. It is a great asset to a centre if he can change direction on the run, without materially reducing his speed even for a moment; whilst it is also a good thing if he can, at a flash, work up from half-speed to full speed. This is of great use when he has gone through on his own, and he wants to get quite clear before his opponents come after him. It enables him to get further from them at once, and it also enables him to work up a better position for his wing, who will probably have come along to back him up, and who will be a faster man than himself.

On the defence, as has been said, the centre must be able to tackle, to stop rushes, and to kick. He must watch his *vis-á-vis*, and make up his mind in an instant, as soon as his opponents have got under way, whom he is going to fetch down. Immediately the ball goes to the opposing forwards in the scrum, he should close up on the scrum so as to give the opposing backs as little room as possible to work in, and then he should make for the man he has marked out, with all speed, timing it so that he reaches his man as soon as he possibly can after the latter has received the ball.

The two centres, together with the scrum half, are always looked upon as players who should do the bulk of the defensive work in midfield, so that there should be no such thing for a centre as "buying the dummy" or failing to go down to a rush. In kicking, he should also indulge in plenty of practice with a wet ball. Many a good kicker with a dry ball has failed lamentably with a wet one. A man who can kick a wet ball with any judgment as to length – and direction is a tremendous asset to his side, and in this respect I have never seen the superiors of J. T. Taylor (Durham and England) and W. J. A. Davies.

I have not gone more fully into the play of a centre threequarter because so much that he has to do is similar to the work of an outside half; so I should advise anybody who wishes to play in the centre to read all that has been said in the chapter on the play of the outside half.

7

Threequarter Play (Part Two)

THE WING THREEQUARTERS

A wing need not have the physique of a centre: in fact, he rarely has. There is much less hard defensive work to be done by a wing; in addition to which he must, above all things, be fast, especially for about fifty yards. Needless to say, fast men are often big men, and make splendid wings despite being big. Again, big men often compensate for a comparative lack of speed by their superior dash. A. Hudson, who played on the wing for England in 1906 and 1908, weighed just over thirteen stone when at his best. His greatness as a wing lay in the superb dash with which he went for the line. He was practically unstoppable when he got the ball twenty yards from the line, and during the 1906 season he scored forty-one times for Gloucester. But I must confess to a liking for a fairly light man on the wing, about ten and a half stone, say. A man of that weight, possessed of plenty of speed and grit, ought, if he has the temperament, to make a splendid wing.

C. N. Lowe, E. T. Morgan, the late J. G. Will, G. B. Crole, G. C. Robinson, and the late Reggie Forrest are the type I have in mind – fast, plucky, and nippy in the extreme. Men who are very fast on the track have rarely done well on the Rugby field. Track running and running as part of a game of Rugby football are totally different, and even when the physical attributes necessary for both are possessed by the same individual, rarely has he the right temperament for both. "Even-timers" have risen to be Internationals – A. E. Hind (England) is a case in point; but never has a flier of this kind been a really great wing. The essential part of a wing's speed is that he shall be a quick starter, and that he shall be able to run about forty yards brilliantly. Very rarely is he required to go further, but he must be prepared to do these forty-yard bursts at a great speed. If a man thinks, then, that he would like to become a second C. N. Lowe, he must first practise bursts of twenty to fifty yards on grass, and in football attire.

A wing threequarter is very much of an individual player. In most cases he is called upon to finish off a movement with nobody to support him, and the idea of combination should enter his mind only after he is quite convinced that he cannot get through on his own. Latterly, the obsession of combined play has overcome wings to a ridiculous extent, and one has seen these men, primarily individualistic players, immediately on receiving the ball, preparing to pass it back to the centre! This is surely another case of "combination gone mad." Generally speaking, then, a wing should regard himself as given the ball to do what he can with it on his own. Just before the ball reaches him, he should size up the disposition of his opponents, and quickly decide upon the tactics he is going to adopt to get behind them. The easiest way, if it is possible, is to run round them by means of his superior speed. Whether this is possible depends largely on his own speed and the previous play of his centre, or whoever gives him the ball, for the latter person should have arranged his play and timed his pass so as to leave the wing man with a chance of getting round his opponent or opponents. It will help the wing if he can gather the ball quickly – with his left arm if he is a right wing, and with his right arm if he is a left wing; for if he can do this smartly and surely, it will take less time and interfere less with his stride than if he uses two hands. In addition, he must try not to check himself when the pass comes to him: a single falter may make all the difference between getting clear and getting tackled. Assuming that he takes his pass perfectly, he must go at full speed around his opponents, making his course as direct towards his opponents' goal-line rather than the touch-line, as is compatible with his rounding the man or men in front of him. Probably three-fourths of all tries scored by wings are obtained in this way.

It may be that the wing is clear of all but the full-back when he gets possession, so that his sole object is to beat that one man – not an easy task if the full-back is a Gamlin or a Johnson or a Lyon. If the wing is left in possession under these circumstances in midfield (that is, the full-back is in the vicinity of the line of the goal-posts), the best plan is for him to make for one of the corners, relying upon his speed to take him past the full-back. The danger to be avoided in this manoeuvre is that of the wing's showing too soon the direction in which he is going. If he does this, it will enable the full-back to run across and catch him, for the full-back will have less distance to run than the wing. The wing should run straight at the full-back for some distance, and then when he sees that he is the proper distance away – and the correct estimation of this distance only comes by practice he should cut away in the direction he intends going, keeping as wide of the full-back as he can, as long as he is making headway towards the opponents' goal-line, and relying upon his speed to get him past the full-back.

Another way to beat a full-back is as follows: – The wing is in possession and is running up to the full-back, who is stationary somewhere in midfield. The wing when well away from the full-back makes off for one of the corners. The full-back will cut across after him. When the wing sees that the full-back is well under way, the former suddenly changes direction and cuts inside the full-back.

The precautions to take here are: –

1. To make sure that you have deceived the full-back by making him come "all out" after you; and

2. That you change your direction at the right moment, not too soon, or you will give the full-back time to pull up and tackle you, or too late, when an outstretched arm may impede you or even fetch you down.

The root principle of beating a stationary full-back is that you must get him on the run, and then either run round him or cut in behind him. The short punt over the full-back's head is another manoeuvre often used, the idea being that the wing will race him for the ball, as the full-back has to turn round and work up speed, whereas the wing is going at full speed all the time. Only a man who is convinced that he cannot possibly beat the full-back in any other way should try the short punt. It is a bad method. There is the difficulty of judging the length and direction of the kick when going at full speed, and also the uncertainty of the bounce. Moreover, it is bad Rugby to lose possession of the ball, when there is a possibility of doing good with it whilst retaining it in your own possession. There are occasions, obviously, when the short punt must be used, *e.g.* when the full-back is one, of those rare beings who seem to hypnotise the wing as he rushes towards him, and almost to induce the wing to run into his arms.

H. T. Gamlin (Devon Albion, Blackheath, and England) was the best example of this wonderful power that I have ever seen. His was a true Verdun-like attitude: – "*On ne passera pas!*" This short punt must be well timed, and the wing must go his very hardest when running to field the ball, so as to race the full-back. It will materially assist the wing if he has had plenty of practice at fielding cleanly a rolling ball, because he won't have much time in which to pick it up. Again, the wing may have to use this short punt if he is hemmed in close to the touch-line by a number of his opponents. But, though it is one of his weapons, I should strongly advise a wing to keep it only for the peculiar conditions when it is suitable.

I remember seeing the late J. G. Will adopting a capital ruse against us at Gloucester when playing for the O. M. T.'s. He was going down the field, about ten yards from the touch-line, and our full back – a splendid tackler – was coming across to cut him off. The full-back had gauged his pace to reach Will at a certain spot, when to his, and our, astonishment Will changed his pace just before reaching that spot, increasing it by about ten yards in a hundred. This enabled him to flash past the full-back before the latter could reach him, and Will scored in the corner. The other O. M. T. wing of that day, E. J. O'Callaghan, was also very clever at this trick – one that takes a lot of doing, but is very effective when well done.

Then, again, who that saw England draw with Ireland at Twickenham in 1910 – a match notable for the fact that R. A. Lloyd made his first appearance for Ireland and for the fact that a really fine English side could only draw with a poor Irish side – will ever forget F. E. Chapman's glorious side-stepping? One run, in particular, when he beat at least a half a dozen Irishmen by side-stepping them in quick succession, was perfectly amazing. It needs a very agile man to side-step well, for it has to be done when going at a fair speed, and at a time when the actual side-stepping will take you right behind your opponents. The nippy wing must keep that also in mind as a means of getting past opponents.

Another method of beating men that has been practised by some wings, especially those on the strong side, is the "hand-off." It consists of a jab, with a stiff arm, at the shoulders, chest, or chin of a man who goes high for the wing, and when done properly sends the would-be tackler flat on his back as a rule. V. H. Coates (Bath, Cambridge, and England) was a splendid exponent of this method, and his feats in 1912 will not soon be forgotten. Obviously it is useless to try this unless the tackler goes for the wing high up, but when this is the case, the hand-off is certainly the best way to elude a tackle, especially if the wing is on the slow side. The wing ought not to pull up too much to hand-off; he will have to do so slightly, but it must not be too pronounced, or he will probably be tackled by some pursuer other than the one he is trying to hand-off.

These, then, are a few ways in which a wing threequarter can beat men "on his own." With them all he must be absolutely whole-hearted in his work, and, especially when the effort is being made near the opposing goal-line, he should fling himself into the effort with the utmost abandon, realising that dash by itself will carry a man past weak opposition, and that dash added to skill will overcome practically any opposition. A big wing will use more dash than skill as a rule, and he will expect to brush by feeble opposition, so that he must be more determined in this work than anyone. Hudson scored dozens of tries by the fear he instilled into his would-be tacklers, as they saw him coming down the field, teeth set, knees high, and "brute force" writ large all over him.

In combination with the other threequarters, and the rest of the team, the wing must always be on the look-out to see whether he is being supported, on the inside or the outside, by a man better placed than himself, and he must also realise that if he is quite cut off by opponents racing him to the touch line, he will be expected to punt across for the rest of the team to follow up and get possession in midfield, and probably behind their opponents. The pass inside is often resorted to when the short (or blind) side is worked. It is also used when the centre follows his wing after passing to him in an open-side movement. Anyone who tries this pass back will see at once how difficult it is to prevent the ball from going forward; but practice will work wonders, though the very best players get the inside pass forward more often than not. When done properly, it is always wonderfully effective, for it enables the receiver to cut diagonally across and behind his opponents. What the wing must avoid is to think of this pass as soon as he receives the ball: it must never be used until the wing has done all he can with the ball. Sometimes, after close work, a centre can dodge round and get outside his wing, so as to be in a position to take an outside pass. Especially does this happen when the wing has had to work his way inwards rather than outwards.

Very few can exploit the cross punt with any skill, but it is well worth practising. Had either of the Cambridge wings been able to do this properly, and had there been some sort of understanding with the forwards as to when this was going to be done, I don't think the Light Blues would have lost the Varsity match of 1921. I saw a striking illustration of the value of the cross-punt in a match some years ago. Wales were playing Ireland at Swansea in 1901. The Irish forwards, among whom were the wonderful Brothers Ryan, and who were ably backed up by Louis Magee and J. J. Coffey at half, simply swamped the Welsh pack in the first half and crossed over with a lead of three tries to nil, all the scores being due to fine forward play. In the second half, the Welsh forwards made a better show and were able to keep their opponents out; but the Welshmen never looked like scoring until Vivian Huzzey, the right wing, brought the cross punt into play. On two occasions when he was all but forced into the touch-line after running up the field, he cross-kicked with excellent judgment. The forwards had anticipated this, and were ready to take advantage of the kick. A forward fielded the ball from a bounce, there was a sharp bout of passing, and a try followed each time. The positions were favourable, and W. J. Bancroft converted, with the result that Wales won by two converted goals to three tries. In fairness to Ireland, though, I ought to say that on both occasions the Welsh forwards were in front of the kicker when he cross-punted, but, fortunately for them, the referee did not see them or the scores would not have been allowed, for they were yards offside. I can see Magee leaning against the upright now, in disgust at the referee's allowing the scores.

The Swansea team that went through the season of 1906 without a defeat was another side that brought this trick off well, the collusion between W. J. Trew and the pack being admirable. A wing should use the cross-punt when he sees that he is bound to be forced into touch or tackled in a few yards, and that so many of the defence are in his neighbourhood, that a cross-kick will enable him to get the ball past most of his opponents and into a position where his forwards can follow up and gain possession. It should be clearly understood by the forwards of a team, that as soon as they see a back movement working towards one side of the field, some of them should dash up the centre of the field, always remembering to keep behind the man in possession of the ball, ready for the cross kick. (I have referred to this also in the chapters on "Forward Play.") A wing must not, however, develop a cross-kick mania – an easy disease to catch. As I have said before, do all you can with the ball in your possession, and only kick it when you cannot do any more with it yourself or by passing.

There is another method of beating a man that I must mention, though not one wing in fifty will be able to do it with success. Still, it was done brilliantly by a famous player, and should consequently be considered. I mean jumping over the full-back! Who will ever forget S. F. Coopper (Blackheath and England) and his "jumps"? Suppose he were bearing for the right corner. He would go at top speed with the full-back coming across to cut him off. At the right moment the full-back would leap at Coopper's legs.

Timing the action beautifully, the wing would jump over the shoulders and outstretched arms of his opponent, clear him, and continue his run like a well-trained hurdler. "He will break his neck one day!" was the cry one always heard when Coopper had "cleared" his man. But he never did, nor was he ever seriously hurt by this manoeuvre, and he is still fit and keen, training the younger element in the Royal Navy to play Rugby.

On the defence, the wing's principal duty is to watch his opponent and to bring him to earth as soon as possible after his receiving the ball. He must remember all the various tricks he himself would use to beat his man, and he must judge from the circumstances which trick is likely to be played against him. Too often one sees wings who are splendid on the attack, but frightfully weak at tackling. This ought not to be. I have never seen better wings than C. N. Lowe and E. T. Morgan, and what magnificent tacklers, though they were both decidedly small men! Then a wing will find kicking useful for his defence, so that he should practise finding touch whilst on the run, and whilst close to the touch-line.

A tendency I have noticed with wings is to stray all over the field. The result is that they often earn rounds of applause from the crowd for doing work which another player, whose task it really was, would have done quite as well; but when it comes to backing up their centres to finish off a movement, especially from a snap chance that has occurred in some loose play, they are nowhere to be found. One finds this generally when a very keen player is a member of a poor side. He is so anxious to do well for his side that he is here, there, and everywhere, and gets a tremendous reputation. This often leads to his being chosen for his county, a "Trial," or even his country, and he lets them down badly by not being in his place at a critical moment. There was one outstanding case of this some years ago, the player concerned – an international, by the way – being one of the most whole-hearted fellows one could meet. A wing should keep to his place, leaving it to assist in the defence elsewhere only when he feels practically certain that the attacking movement of his opponents will not come his way, and that he won't weaken his side's defence or attack by leaving his position. He must remember, too, that his place is known to his opponents, and that if he is seen playing out of his position, a shrewd side will try to divert the attack to where the wing should have been.

In a sense, I regard the wing position as one of the most comfortable on the field. The wing does not as a rule have much hard work to do in the way of tackling and rush-stopping, whilst he is almost certain to have a few chances of rounding off a passing movement, when pace and a little dash will enable him to score. But the ideal wing needs to be armed at all points, and should attend at least to the points outlined above.

8

Full-Back Play (Part One)

THE FULL-BACK

This player forms the last line of defence, so his responsibility is a heavy one. Very seldom does one see a game in which the full-back has not, single-handed, to keep the other side from scoring. Sometimes he is confronted with just one opponent; more often with numbers of them, in support of the man in possession. What a glorious sensation for a man to prevent the other side from scoring under these circumstances! Obviously, then, one of the most valuable assets a full-back can possess is coolness. He must be able to take in the situation at a glance, to decide on his tactics at once, and to put them into practice with the utmost skill and vigour he can command, and yet to do so without any flurry. What is more, he must be prepared to change his tactics in a flash, if a new manoeuvre is tried by the opposition. Steady he must be, with no trace of nervousness or confusion.

There is such a thing as being too cool, though, which is almost as bad as getting excited or worried under pressure. This may be prompted by the same motive as makes the nervous boy whistle and sing as he goes through a dark country lane at night, *viz.* so as to persuade himself that he isn't afraid, *à la Coue-ism*. Sometimes, on the other hand, this ultra-coolness is a pose, designed to appeal to the spectators – a horrible motive! The ideal is perfect self-control, which is largely temperamental (the highly-strung individual should not dream of playing full-back), though it can be developed to a surprising extent. It is very helpful for a full-back who is standing waiting, whilst his opponents are working towards his line, to breathe slowly and deeply. This steadies the nerves wonderfully. I have taken this aspect of a full-back's play first because it is all-important to him. He can never be a reliable last line of defence if he is not cool under pressure. What is more, watchful side always "spots" an excitable full-back, and gives him every opportunity to get flurried by letting him have plenty of high punts to field, with the forwards well-nigh on top of him, and by dashing down to him, in a forward rush, say, with the utmost determination written on their faces. These tactics, however, are not tried more than once on a man who obviously loves a tight corner, and does better the harder he is pressed. Rugby was not played in his time, I am afraid, but Horace has aptly described our model full-back, as far as temperament is concerned, when he says in one of his famous odes, of a steadfast man:

> *Si fractus inlabatur orbis,*
> *Inpavidum ferient ruinae.*

After coolness, I think I should recommend a budding full-back to develop a safe pair of hands. He will get all sorts of balls to field: high punts, long raking kicks, and nasty bouncing balls – the most difficult of all to take. Each and every one he must learn to field quickly and cleanly: there must be no wobbling of the ball in his hands or arms before he has it firmly in his possession. He must practise taking the ball in the air, with a kind of cradle made by the palms of the hands, the forearms, and the body. At the moment of impact he must give with his arms and body slightly, so that the ball won't rebound. Above all, he must not let the tips of his fingers touch the ball, for if they do the ball will almost certainly slip away from him, to say nothing of the likelihood of his hurting his fingers (many a full-back has broken his fingers in that way).   This art of fielding a ball in the air is easily acquired by practice, and a full-back cannot be too sure at it. Closely bound up with that art, is that of judging the flight of a ball. Rarely has the full-back not to move to field the kick, and he must assiduously practise judging the flight of a ball, so that, be it far off or near, he can regulate his pace in order to reach it at the right second. If this is not done, he will have the chagrin of seeing the ball drop in front of him, or will have to hasten his pace for the last few strides. Should the ball drop in front of him, his position is hopeless, for the chances are that the ball will bounce over his head or on one side of him, and his opponents will soon get past him. If he has to hasten his speed, he is likely to reach the ball in a flurried state, which means that he will probably drop it. It is a most fascinating art, that of being able to field the ball from any sort of kick, and it looks so easy when well done! But it takes hours of practice to make it easy.

A full-back will be well advised to spend some time in training, at learning to field a ball when on the run, and to continue the run after taking the ball, checking himself as little as possible. This is much more difficult; yet the ability to do it has often enabled a full-back to start a movement that has led to a score, and sometimes to his scoring on his own. A. F. Marsburg, the South African full-back of 1906, was a marvellous fellow at this. He had an uncanny knack of making a wild dash for a ball, twenty or thirty yards away, reaching it when at the top of his speed, holding it securely, and continuing to run at full speed. It was a most exhilarating sight, and always sent the crowds into ecstasies. Needless to say, if any men were in the vicinity of the ball when he took it, over they went, did he touch them on the way, for he was not a small man, and with this momentum he took some checking. Sometimes he would finish up with a mighty punt up the field, whilst at other times he would set his backs going. A most daring exhibition of this kind of fielding led to his being carried off the field at Swansea after the Wales *v.* South Africa match in 1906 by the enthusiastic Welsh spectators. Few players will become Marsburgs, for temperament enters largely into this "field-and-follow-through" idea, but it is worth practising. Again, a full-back must learn to pick up a ball – coming towards him, or going away from him, rolling along the ground, or bouncing clumsily as only a Rugby ball can – with absolute certainty. I have said it before, and I repeat it: a full-back cannot be too sure a fielder, and he must give his nights and days to it, as it were, for if he is an uncertain fielder, he had better change his position.

Not only does this sure fielding materially affect the individual value of the full-back, but it considerably affects the play of the other members of the side. With a sure fielder behind them the members of a team don't get the slightest bit worried when the ball is kicked over their heads. They know that it will be cleanly taken, and something useful done with the ball probably. On the other hand, if a full-back is an uncertain fielder, the rest of the side are on tenterhooks if the ball passes them. They begin to go back to support him, and by their worry reduce their value on the attack or the defence, for the time, by a good deal. It was my fortune to play in front of some superb fielders, *e.g.* George Romans (Gloucester), W. R. Johnson (Gloucestershire and England), A. E. Wood (Gloucester and England), and E. J. Jackett (Leicester and England). Never did the sides for whom these men played worry when the ball went to them. They knew that it would be taken and held first time, and probably returned with not a little interest! I have seen full-backs in club football do quite well, season after season, with these two qualities only in any marked degree, *viz.* a capacity for keeping cool and an ability to field a ball well.

The finest fielder of a kick that I have seen in the past year or two has been H. H. Forsayth (Oxford and Scotland), and I will mention the England-Scotland match of 1922 as only one instance of a marvellous display of clever fielding by him. One last piece of advice on fielding: whatever you do, don't let the ball bounce before you field it, unless you are absolutely forced to do so. Judge the distance quickly; and if it is humanly possible to reach the ball and take it in the air, do so. If it is not, watch the ball carefully and approach it near enough to take it first bounce, if you can, whichever way it goes – and you will have to keep your wits about you to do that!

The full-back should be a good kick – that goes without saying. At punting especially should he be an adept. He will find that this is done with the instep, and steady practice will soon add yards to his length and improve his direction. As this can be done in training, there is no excuse for a man not doing it well. Two or three of the backs should arrange to get on to the ground together and then they could practise punting to each other, which would enable them to improve their fielding at the same time. Then a capital plan is for the full-back to practise finding touch, by taking kicks from varying distances from the touch-line itself, in every case landing the ball over the touch-line at the furthest possible point from where he kicked. He must practise this with both feet, though naturally he will attain a much greater proficiency with one than the other. Finding touch will be the object of three-fourths of his kicks, so he should be able to do this when on the run, and with plenty of length.

In connection with finding touch, a full-back should always edge away from the touch-line as far as possible before putting in his kick. The reason is obvious – it is easier to find touch well up the field when the kicker is twenty yards away from the touch-line, than when he is five. Consequently, as soon as he fields the ball he should go up the field as far as he can, and bear away to the open as much as he can, before he actually puts in his kick. How often does one see a full-back field an attempt to find touch, about five yards, and sometimes less, from the touch-line, and then at once try to find touch himself from that spot, when he could have easily come out into the open and gone some distance up the field! Sheer thoughtlessness, and yet it has been the rule rather than the exception. Also in connection with this art of finding touch crops up the question, which is the better foot to use in kicking to the right touch-line, the right foot or the left? Theoretically, of course, it should be the left foot, as being further from the touch-line – the right foot for the left line, and the left foot for the right line. And this is the best rule to adopt. But a man strong with his right foot, and comparatively weak with his left (for full-backs are only human, and this will be the state of most of them) will try to manoeuvre to use his right foot whenever he can, whilst a brainy side will equally carefully try to let him have the ball in such a position that he can use his "strong" foot with precious little advantage to his side.

In this connection, I well remember a brilliant left-footed full-back of my time, who was guaranteed to find touch sixty yards up the field from any reasonable position, if he could only use his left foot, whereas it was a miserable twenty yards' shot that was the result if he were forced to use his right foot. It was always an understood thing with us that if we were forced to kick down to him it was to be on his right side, and we were to bear towards him so that he could not veer towards his left to use that foot in kicking. By such tactics as these are matches won.

The full-back should also be able to drop-kick well – again an art that can easily be attained in practice. Many players, I believe, use the toe for this kind of kick, though for the snap-kicking I used to do when in the neighbour-hood of the goalposts I always used my instep. One seemed to be able to get better direction, though I must confess there was a decided tendency for the ball to keep low, that had to be guarded against. Again, one must develop the ability to use both feet in turn, and to kick when on the move. Many opportunities occur for a full-back to drop at goal from some open play, whilst if he is the best drop-kick in the side, he is called upon to take the drops for goal after a penalty and to take the drops-out after a touch-down. A drop-kick is sometimes substituted for a punt, in finding touch. It is very effective when kicking to touch against a wind. One gets more distance with a forceful drop-kick of low trajectory than with a punt. I saw B. S. Cumberlege do this often with splendid success during the 1921–22 season.

PLACE-KICKING

A word here might be interposed about place-kicking, a phase of kicking that is sadly neglected nowadays, and one which should be practised by a full-back. Often, though not always, the full-back is expected to take the place-kicks, be they from penalties or efforts to convert tries, and very rarely indeed does one see a game in which a good place-kicker does not have at least one chance of showing his prowess. What is more, every season dozens of matches are won, and of course lost, by place-kicks, so that it behoves all captains to see that some of their team can place-kick well. A player should practise taking shots at goal from all angles in his opponents' half. I think W. J. Bancroft (Wales) was the finest place-kick I have ever seen, and it would be interesting to know how many goals he actually kicked for Swansea and Wales. No matter what the state of the ground was, there was always a reasonable hope of his getting a goal from any spot ten yards inside his opponents' half. Another splendid place-kick was George Romans (Gloucester). In our 1905–06 season, when we had a capital side at Gloucester, he converted seventy tries and kicked three penalty goals with place-kicks – 149 points, a wonderful record. Both these players were full-backs, and most of the good place-kicks I have known have been players in that position (the most brilliant exception was Douglas Morkel, the South African forward, who beat England by his place-kicking at Twickenham in 1913), hence my advice to full-backs to try to make themselves proficient at that art. Strangely enough, many players find themselves more able to place-kick at an angle than from directly in front. Again, some players are wonderfully accurate at "directly-in-front" shots. In the 1921–22 Blackheath side, if my memory serves me rightly, H. Coverdale took all the "in front" shots, and B. S. Cumberlege the oblique shots. It is a moment well worth living for, to be called up from full-back to take a penalty or a conversion from a difficult position, and, with the stage splendidly set for an individual display, owing to the non-participation of practically all the rest of the side, to send the ball beautifully over the cross-bar.

A full-back should bear in mind that kicking to touch may be used not only to save his own forwards a lot of running about, but also to wear down the opposing pack. As I have said earlier in the book, nothing wears forwards down so effectively as sending the ball back fifty yards after they have followed up in the hope that they will tackle the full-back in possession. A trick of W. J. Bancroft's was an improvement upon this. For a sprint of not more than forty yards he was one of the fastest men that ever played. What was more, he was a marvellously sure fielder and touch-finder. When a kick came to him he used to bear off towards one of the touch-lines at a fair speed, but slow enough to encourage the oncoming forwards to think that with an "all-out" effort they would probably catch him. Then, after running like this for about twenty yards, he would increase his speed, get clear, and finish up with a raking shot that sent the ball into touch about fifty yards up the field. This would be varied by his dashing off in one direction for ten or fifteen yards, turning sharply on his heel, and going the opposite way. Imagine the plight of the following-up forwards! By half time they had had more than enough running about, and the side Bancroft was playing for found the opposing forwards much more easy to beat after that. This trick takes a lot of doing, for if the full-back who attempts it is either tackled in possession or else fails to find touch, he is smothered in curses and rightly!

There is another objection to this clever manoeuvre, and this objection is so strong a one, to my mind, that I was reluctant to mention the manoeuvre. I have done so, however, because I expect every Rugby player to be able to use a fair manoeuvre in a sensible way. That objection is that this manoeuvre so often leads a full-back to "play to the gallery": a weak-minded player cannot resist the temptation to earn rounds of applause by giving a dashing pack a brisk run of about thirty yards, only to finish up by sending them back fifty yards nearer their own line. Even W. J. Bancroft found this temptation irresistible at times – so I thought, at least. There is another danger: if you do get tackled, look out! Forwards who have been led round the field twenty times in an afternoon without catching their man will for certain be exasperated enough when they do get hold of him to tackle him with some vigour. The full-back just mentioned was rarely tackled, but the Irish forwards did get hold of him once at Cardiff in an Ireland *v.* Wales game, and they showed no mercy.

A full-back should help his side by every fair means at his command. If he can reduce the effectiveness of the opposing pack by the above manoeuvre he should certainly try it now and then; but I advise him to do so only occasionally, and to remember that a full-back tackled in possession, when he could have parted with the ball advantageously, has committed an unpardonable crime, so to speak. Finally, for goodness' sake, give the trick up at once if you find your weaker self responding to the "call of the gallery."

A HARD TACKLE

9
Full-Back Play (Part Two)

There is not much doubt but that the full-back should be the best tackler in the team. The man he gets his hands on must come to earth and must be made to part with the ball. Around the hips is the ideal place to collar a man, and there is no glory in Rugby to equal that of real hard, but clean, tackling. I think the most thrilling sight I have ever seen was when H. T. Gamlin was at his best, and was bringing down man after man with his octopus-like tackle. We hear a lot of talk nowadays about opening out the game, and so making it more attractive. In their desire to do this, it seems to me that many players have for gotten the art of tackling. They apparently think it doesn't matter if they let a man or two go by, for they will presently have a chance of showing their opponents that they can do as well, if not better. The result has been that the attempts to tackle are often ludicrous, the physical force expended by the would-be tackler being insufficient to disturb the symmetry of a cobweb. No full-back can afford to be other than a good tackler, if he wants to be a real all-rounder. I add the last clause advisedly, for I have known even international full-backs who have been miserable tacklers; but they were brilliant at some other aspects of full-back play.

Now the best way to tackle anybody is from the side. You should contrive to get at him from the side at all costs. Then when you are abreast of him, leap with all your force at his hips, so that you lock your arms tightly round his thighs just below the hips. The impetus with which you do this will in nine cases out of ten bowl the man over. (I need hardly say that you should try to get your head behind the man when you grip him.) After you have got him down, make him play the ball: no tackle is complete unless the man is brought to earth vigorously and held there until he loses the ball. Don't be gentle about this tackling, or you will be shaken off. The instant before you leap, make up your mind that you will put all your force into the leap, and then hold on to the man with a vice-like grip, thus making it impossible, since you are holding his legs, for him to go any further. If your man is coming straight towards you and it seems impossible to take him from the side, the best thing to do is either to dash at his insteps in the manner suggested for rushstopping, or else to recede a yard or two so as to get him from the side eventually. It doesn't matter a bit how small the tackler is, or how big the man in position is; tackled properly the latter should be stopped every time. In some ways it is easier for the small man to tackle well: for one thing, it is much more difficult to hand-off a small man.

Generally speaking, it is an unpardonable sin to attempt to tackle a man high. Sometimes, however, when a full-back wants to prevent the man he has tackled from passing the ball, he will go high, in order to "smother" the man and the ball. For instance, suppose a couple of men are coming down the field with the full-back only in front of them. The full-back knows that if the man he is going to tackle has any skill at all he will endeavour to induce the full-back to tackle him the merest fraction of a second after he has passed the ball to his partner. Under those circumstances, the full-back should try to tackle the man with the ball in such a way and at such a time that the latter will not be able to pass to the man supporting him. To do this the full-back should watch his man carefully and spring at him just below the shoulders as he is about to pass. If the tackle is done properly the passer's arms are pinned to his side, and he is powerless to let his partner have the ball. The first duty of a full-back is to bring down the man with the ball – that is fundamental. In most cases the latter will have passed just before he was tackled. If the full-back brings down the man and the ball, when the latter had men in support ready to take his pass, he has done more than well. I have seen very plucky full-backs who were generally considered good tacklers give away many tries through thoughtlessness, under the following circumstances. An attack is made on their line from fairly close in, and they stand on or very close to their own goal-line to check the movement. What happens? They tackle the man in possession right enough, but the momentum of the latter enables him to fall over the line, and a try is the result, despite the tackle. A full-back should always glance at his position when he is very close to his own line, and, if necessary, take a pace or two up the field, so as to get the full benefit of any tackle he may bring off.

An advanced form of tackling is what is known as the deferred tackle. Suppose that after a bout of passing down the right side of the field, the right centre and the right wing were clear of everybody but the full-back, and were, say, forty yards from the goal-line and about thirty from the touchline. If the full-back made straight for the centre at once he would in all probability tackle him, out the latter would pass to his wing, who would have a clear run-in. On the other hand, if the full-back could cover the centre on the latter's left, and keep forcing him to go towards the touch-line, he might induce the centre to hold on until he had bored his wing so close to the touch-line as to make it extremely difficult for the wing to get by the full-back in the limited space at his disposal; or he might, by this delay, enable a member of his own side to cut across and take the wing man, which he would never have done had the full-back not deferred his tackle. In my time no man has equalled H. T. Gamlin at this clever manoeuvre. Not once, but dozens of times, have I seen Gamlin confronted by three threequarters bearing obliquely to their left, we'll say, and Gamlin has so hypnotised the man with the ball as to induce him to go on and on towards the touch-line, only to see the other centre and wing threequarter forced so close together that when the ball has gone to the second centre, he and the wing have been bowled over together and into the touch-line. W. J. Trew was another player who practised this and taught it to others. I don't recommend any youngster to defer his tackle in this way until he is very sure of himself. But as he gets more experienced he should try it in practice games to see whether he can do it with safety. If not – and the vast majority of full-backs will never do it well – he had better be content with admiring those who can do it, and satisfy himself with fetching his man down at the first opportunity.

A full-back should always bear in mind that when he is confronted with a player who has broken clean away, and has only him to beat, his best plan is to stand still as long as he can. The sooner he moves towards either his right or left the more easily will he be beaten, for, as has been said in the chapter on wing play, the object of a wing when he has only the full-back to beat is to get the latter to move in one direction, and then for him, the wing, to go in the other. Well, the countermove for the full-back is to stand still, or nearly so, as long as he can, and only to go "all out" for his man when he is as certain as he can be of the direction in which the wing is going. It is extraordinary the effect that this has on a wing. Often he seems hypnotised by the full-back and falls an easy prey to him by making a poor attempt to get by him. The best case I can remember of this was a game in which an International wing got away, with only the full-back in front of him. The latter stood still, about thirty yards away. The wing got worried as he saw the back not moving towards him, so he thought he would try a feint one way and then double back the other. But he did this so far away from the back, and so clumsily at that, that the wing feinted, doubled back, and practically dashed into the arms of the full-back, who had scarcely moved! Incredible it seems, I know; but I advise anybody to try and beat a clever tackler, who is waiting for him, and who resists the attempt made to induce him to get moving in one direction. He won't find it easy.

Another great gift that is possessed by the best full-backs is that of anticipation. As a result of years of experience, and, consequently, a long study of all sorts of moves in the game, these players are able to take in at a glance what is the next move on the board, and are thus able to be more ready to checkmate it when it is done by their opponents, or to assist in it when it is done by their own side. Study the best full-backs at work, and you will see that whatever their opponents are doing they are on the alert, shuffling this way or that, quietly and unostentatiously; so, when the movement does reach them, they are in the most advantageous position to pull it up. It has annoyed me scores of times to see a full-back receive a storm of applause after bringing off a tackle following a twenty yards' dash for the man with the ball; whilst when a full-back who has seen some seconds before what was almost certain to happen and has quietly but quickly got into position and been ready to effect the tackle without any "fireworks" display, the crowd has hardly noticed the tackle. This is always the difference to my mind between a "class" full-back and just a good one, *viz.* the wonderful sense of anticipation possessed by the former, by which ordinary play is made to look easy, and the apparently impossible made possible. Naturally, this sense is developed to the fullest extent after playing for a long time, but one could go on playing for a lifetime and have this gift to a very slight extent did not one do the essential thing, *viz.* watch the game from beginning to end and think about it. That is why I always consider that no full-back should be idle, even though his side is doing all the attacking. To stand back and watch the different manoeuvres by which your side tries to beat your opponents, and to observe at the same time how the latter try to deal with these manoeuvres, is a most engrossing occupation. Moreover, all the knowledge thus acquired is going to supply the solution of most of the difficulties you will have to face.

Generally speaking, the full-back's role is a defensive one; but this must not blind him to his potentialities as an attacking player. Even in the matter of kicking, mainly a defensive operation, he must try to bear in mind that the result of his kick must be to enable his side to attack more strongly. For this reason he must not always kick to touch, although a kick of fifty yards or so up the field is tremendously helpful to a side. There is the cross-kick to be used now and then, when he finds himself on one side of the field with quite a lot of his team well placed in the centre of the field to carry on a carefully judged cross-kick. Again, there is the high punt, supported by sharp following up, which has penetrated many a defence. Especially is this a capital weapon to use when your opponents have a troublesome sun in their eyes. Another useful attacking kick is the one given well up the field to a spot which has been left open by your opponents, and which the fast men of your side are likely to reach before your opponents. All these just show that a full-back must not get obsessed with the idea that every time he gets the ball he must kick to touch. As a general principle, that must be his first consideration, but I have said enough to show that sometimes it is far more advantageous to your side not to kick to touch. Then the full-back can sometimes do good attacking work by

PASSING THE BALL

actually joining the backs in a movement, but I advise all full-backs to be chary about this. Don't let the temptation of a possible try make you too keen on attempting to get one. I would far rather have a safe full-back who left passing movements to the backs, and kept to his right position all the time, than a brilliant sort of man who was likely to score a try for his side now and then, but who would many times let his side down by not being in his position when wanted. For, be sure of this, a brainy side that notices the propensity of a full-back to leave his right place will soon coax him out of it, and so get a clear run in.

There are, however, some occasions when by all the laws of probability a full-back can, with success, join the threequarters and halves in an attack. I have seen a full-back prove of immense value to his side by quietly slipping into a blind-side attack. An extra man in this manoeuvre often makes the difference between a score and no score. In this case, the full-back should conceal his intentions till the last second. He should take up his normal position, and only move from it very slowly at first, actually participating in the movement by a sharp dash at the psychological moment. Again, a full-back who fields a kick must always think whether it is not better to start a bout of passing than to kick. A glance will show him whether there is a splendid opening for a back movement on either side of the field, and he can often start one with safety, after a sharp run up, and then fall back to take up his right position. J. Strand Jones (Oxford and Wales), W. J. Bancroft (Wales), and S. Cumberlege (England) have done this exceedingly well. I have on occasions seen full-backs dash up to one side of the field and form an extra threequarter, centre or wing, at a critical moment in an open-side attack. All these practices are, for a full-back, departures from his normal play, and this he must never forget. If he yields to the temptation of being "abnormal" too often, he is bound to let his side down; so let every full-back shun these tricks until he knows when exactly to use them and has the ability to use them well. I consider full-back the most fascinating position in the team. It was always my desire to play there, and it was only unsuitability of physique that kept me from trying the position seriously. As it was, I played there dozens of times in practice games, and thoroughly enjoyed it. Full-back play has sadly deteriorated since the War, and I hope that any young players in the position will give plenty of time and thought to the game. This will soon raise the standard of play in the position. Coolness, a safe pair of hands, the ability to kick (especially to punt), a knowledge of how to tackle, unlimited pluck, a mind equally alert at sizing up a situation as in deciding upon its solution, ability to run about thirty yards well, and a sense of anticipation these are the main qualities that go to make a full-back, and many of them can be attained by steady practice and thought.

10

The Team as a Whole (Part One)

So far, the basis of all that I have written has been the functions of the various players in a team as individuals, rather than as members of a single whole, though in discussing this individual aspect frequent reference has been made to the support that the various members of a team should expect when performing any manoeuvres. The model side is the one that bases its general play on the idea of combination, but whose several members know that combination is most effectively carried out by occasional resort to sheer individualism. Even though the individual effort often leads to nothing in itself, it must be tried from time to time, in order to keep the opposition guessing whether the man in possession is going on his own, or whether he is going to play to his side. Your opportunity is given to you when you have the defence guessing, and I should think that half the tries that are scored are due to tactics on the part of the attacking side that lead the defence to wonder what is going to happen next. In order to get the benefit of combined play, it is best that every member of the side should have a rough idea of the functions of the various parts of a 1 team – forwards, halves, threequarters, and full-back. This could easily be done by a few talks from a capable captain, especially if he demonstrated his points with a blackboard and chalk, or even with a box of matches on a table – many a strenuous game have I played with matches! Obviously, the various players will not learn

A FREE KICK.

these functions in order to perform them all, but rather to know what exactly is afoot when a movement is started, and how best they can fit in with it and support it by any ability they possess. Nothing looks more ridiculous than for a group of forwards to stand still and watch a back movement in operation, or for a set of backs to look idly on at a forward dribble.

Every movement of a side, whether it is performed by one or more players, should receive the support of the rest of the team. This support should generally take the form either of active participation in the movement itself, or preparation for the subsequent play that is likely to develop from it. For example, an open attack by the backs, bearing towards one corner, should be supported by the forwards bearing up the field, ready to take any inside passes that may result, or to field any cross-kick that may come along. Sometimes active participation is impossible, especially if the play has suddenly developed in a part of the field remote from a player. Under those circumstances, the player should use his sense of anticipation and get into a position where he can be of service if the movement be checked, and his side be called upon to defend. No member of a side must be idle, whether his side is attacking or defending. If he is physically idle for a second or two, as may be sometimes the case, he should be mentally on the alert, watching intently what is going on, and reasoning out quickly what is going to happen next.

As I have said, this idea should be applied to both attack and defence. The sides that do best are invariably those that have this combined idea strongly developed. Every man seems ready to take his part in what is being done; but don't let this be interpreted into everybody getting into everybody else's way, a very possible consequence of this advice. Players should remember that if a movement is being developed by any part of a team, say the threequarters, it is their movement primarily, and the other members of the team should only support it, which means that they should be up and ready to supply extra men if need be, or to carry on the attack if the original movement breaks down. A distorted view of combination has often resulted in fast forwards getting right into the way of centre threequarters or halves, the latter of whom have had precious little room to work in to begin with, whilst with the extra impediment of a well-meaning forward or two the movement cannot possibly be successful. Again, an over-zealous forward will sometimes get up from the back of the scrum if he thinks the half back is not there, and pick up the ball so as to feed the backs. More than one forward has had my vials of wrath poured on him for doing this sort of thing – useless in nineteen cases out of twenty, and better not done in the twentieth case.

The full-back is another person who often suffers from that same evil. Other members of the side will rush back to his support if they see him hard pressed, but when they get near him they forget that they have come to help him, and fancy they have come to do his job for him. Many a time a full-back will be just about to field a ball when another member of his side will come up, and with a shout of "All right!" take the ball almost out of the full-back's hands. It is bad enough if he fields the ball cleanly, for even then it is distracting to have one's work interfered with; but, as a rule, if two men are going for the ball, it means that neither takes it. Again, when a full-back is about to tackle a player, occasionally another man will come up and bring about the tackle just when the full-back is going to take his man. This means that the full-back is useless to his side for that particular movement, as he cannot often adjust his position or mentality quickly enough to check the next move. On the other hand, if the player really wants to support the full-back, he should have got into position to take the man in possession should his full-back have missed him, and

THE DISADVANTAGE OF HURRY—"NO CHARGE"

to be ready to bring down the next man should the man originally in possession have been tackled by the full-back and yet have been able to pass the ball. These are just a few illustrations of the harm that may be done by well-meaning players with a wrong idea of what combination in attack and defence means.

Perfect combination in a side is the result of this knowledge on the part of the individual members of what the functions of all are, together with a knowledge of the idiosyncrasies the various members possess. This latter aspect is important. No Rugby player should be absolutely mechanical in his play: fortunately few are. Nearly everybody has his own particular trick that he likes to bring off, if conditions are favourable, just as every batsman has his own favourite stroke in cricket, and every golfer his favourite shot in that game. If every member of a side knew the circumstances under which a man brought into play his favourite trick, and could be in position to support the player in question or to lead up to his trick, that side would be a very hot one. That is why club sides do so well, and, a better example still, touring sides. It may be assumed that the members of an international side all know what the functions of a half, a threequarter, a full-back, and a forward are – though I know I am generous to many internationals in saying this! – and they should consequently be able to support the normal movements of attack and defence. But where they lack the extra combination of the club or touring side is in the knowledge of the strong points of certain members of the side, when they scorn the conventional and go on their own. Any follower of the game can call to mind more than one side whose individual members are just ordinary players, with, few or none fit for higher honours, which has had a most successful season because the members of the team seem so absolutely enrapport with their ideas. The touring side, naturally, has greater advantages even than the club side, for the former generally plays a couple of matches every week, and so has twice as many chances of seeing each other's strengths and weaknesses. A striking case of this was the Australian team of 1908. There were a few splendid players in the side, Tom Richards for one; but on the whole they were just ordinary club players. Yet they lost only five of the thirty matches they played, and even beat England by nine points to three, whilst they ran Wales to three points: There are other factors that work in favour of a touring side, I know, but the greatest asset is the knowledge of one another's idiosyncrasies that they obtain by the close succession of the numerous games they play.

This latter aspect of combination, *viz.* playing to the strength of individual members, implies a certain development of individualism. What are one's pleasantest memories in Rugby? The feats of individuals, surely. The tackling of H. T. Gamlin and W. R. Johnson, the swerving of the late Ronald Poulton and W. J. Trew, the amazing sense of anticipation in W. J. Bancroft and E. J. Jackett, the glorious bursts of the late Basil Maclear (Ireland), Kenneth Macleod (Scotland), and Gwyn Nicholls, the dashes from the scrum of C. A. Kershaw, the beautiful drop-kicking of W. J. A. Davies and P. F. Bush, the fielding of the ball by A. F. Marsburg, the determination of A. Tedford (Ireland), A. L. Kewney (England), John Daniell (England), the late "Darkie" Sivright (Scotland), Seeling (New Zealand), and A. F. Harding (Wales) in going for the line, the side-stepping of F. E. Chapman, and the elusiveness of C. N. Lowe, E. T. Morgan, and the late J. G. Will are just a few of my pleasantest recollections of the game. Rugby would degenerate sadly if the idea of combination were to discourage the individual tendencies of geniuses, which many of those I have named undoubtedly were. A player should soon get to know whether there is any trick that he is able to do exceptionally well, and he should set about developing it more highly still, and then (what is equally important) he should constantly be on the watch for the very set of circumstances in a game that will give him the opportunity of bringing off that trick. All the time he should realise two things: –

1. That the cleverest of tricks ceases to be clever if indulged in so often and so patently that the other side knows exactly when to expect it. Would Ronald Poulton have done so well with his elusive swerve if he had not frequently run quite straight? Would F. E. Chapman have side-stepped so many players if they had never been able to tell whether he was going in a direct line or going to side-step? The individual, then, must know the circumstances when he can best bring into play his strength, and even then he must be prepared not to do so occasionally, for fear the opposition will get to know that the trick will be attempted under these circumstances.

2. Then, primarily, he must remember that he is a member of a side, all of whose members must work together to produce the best results. This will mean that in most cases he will be just a unit in a movement, his duty being to play perhaps a small part before passing the ball to someone else whose play is necessary for the success of the movement. The outside half who kicks when he should pass, the centre who hangs on to the ball when he should feed his wing, the scrum half who goes on his own when he should start his backs going, the forward who tries to "bullock" his way through a host of opponents when he has men on either side who could probably get through more easily than he, are a few instances of people who seriously decrease the effectiveness of a side by forgetting that there are fifteen players in a team, not one.

A team has to keep carefully in mind the dual aspect of its play, *viz.* as a unit, and as a combination of men some of whom have marked individual ability under certain

BEFORE THE KICK OFF

circumstances. If the former is the predominating one, and the latter idea is strongly encouraged but well kept under control, the team concerned should do well, and, whatever happens, every member of the side should enjoy his football, for the humblest member will realise that he is a cog in the machine, and the "star" members will have chances of crowning the solid and unostentatious play of the others by their occasional individual efforts.

With regard to tactics, most of the normal modes of attack and defence have been dealt with in discussing the duties of the players who are likely to have the largest share in the various movements, but a word here on general team tactics might be useful. For long there prevailed the idea that it was bad Rugby to start an attacking movement between the half way line and your own "25." If ever the ball got to hand in that quarter, it had to be kicked to touch at once. That idea has now been exploded, fortunately, partly as a result of the great development of back play. When a scrum takes place near your own line, obviously it will be risky to give the ball much air as a rule. But even this rule can be broken, and was, of ten, by A. D. Stoop and his famous pre-War Harlequin team for example. One instance of the success of violating this rule comes to my mind at once. It was in a Gloucestershire *v.* Somerset match at Weston-super-Mare in 1909. I was captain of the former county, and we had a splendid side – as a matter of fact six of the team played for England that season. The back division knew each other's play inside out, and what were apparently very risky manoeuvres were attempted, and with complete success. Well, in this match we were fitting into each other's play more smoothly than ever, and everything was coming off for us. We had a scrum not ten yards from our own line, and near the centre of the field. I arranged with my partner and the rest of the backs that we would try a conventional attacking movement towards the right. The ball came out our side and I fed my partner. He gave a short sharp pass to the left centre, who burst through between the opposing centres and then passed to the right centre, who went on to the full-back before giving the right wing a clear run in with a swift pass. Our opponents made a poor attempt to stop us, mainly because they were unprepared for such a movement.

Still, the basis of the ordinary side's play should be that it is safest to confine one's tactics to defence inside one's own "25," and to attack outside it. But every member of the side must be aware of this, for it only needs one member to forget it, and throw out a reckless pass, to reduce the united efforts of the other fourteen to nothing. Supposing a side is pressed into its "25," it should realise that its duty now is to defend, *i.e.* to keep its opponents from crossing the line, and to get the ball out of that quarter. From open play, the normal method of relieving pressure is by kicking to touch. The back who receives the ball should try to get as much distance as possible into his kick. I was going to add to the last sentence "needless to say," but I have not done so, intentionally, for one often sees fellows send the ball straight into touch immediately they get it, and often with a kick that is at right angles to the touch-line, so that they have gained no ground at all. You don't expect to get much time to ponder over these kicks, I will confess, but two things every player should do, if it is likely that he will have to find touch: –

1. He should see exactly where he is standing, and realise what angle he would like to kick at if he has the chance. When your mind is fixed on this angle, you can often get the ball to the desired position without looking at the direction just before making the kick.

2. He should try to improve his position, if possible, before kicking. He may have a chance of going up the field for a few yards, or he may be able to ease off from the touch-line a little, both of which moves will almost certainly make his kick more effective.

Another thing to remember is that often the best defensive kick is the one that doesn't take place! More than once have I seen the ball go to a brainy back in his own "25," with the opposition all after him on the short side. He has encouraged them by starting off in that direction, and by shaping up for a kick to touch. At the last second, however, he has changed his direction, or cut through his opponents and started an attacking movement with his backs on the open side of the field. B. S. Cumberlege and R. C. Pickles (Bristol and England) did this for their clubs on more than one occasion last season, and did it well.

From tight play in the "25," the safest method of defending is by a close dribble towards the touchline; if from a scrum, in the manner detailed in the chapter on forward play, and if from loose play, on the same lines, with the halves in particular taking a prominent part. There is not much need to refer to the aspect of tackling as a means of keeping your opponents out. Sides are inclined to be keen enough on combination in attack, but to forget it in defence, when it is equally important. Successful defence only follows when every member of the side is keenly on the watch and thinking what his opponents are likely to do if they get the ball, is fully aware of the concerted method of defence his side is going to adopt, and knows exactly what is his part in that method of defence.

FORMING A SCRUMMAGE

11

The Team as a Whole (Part Two)

Attack as a means of defence has been referred to above; now we will consider it as a means of breaking through your opponents' defence. Roughly speaking you can attack with your pack, the backs supporting; or with your backs, the pack supporting. With a pack that is overwhelmingly superior, the former plan is the better to adopt; but it is not often possible, though I have mentioned cases in this book – and other cases will at once occur to many readers – where it was possible, and enabled the side to win, where the superiority of the pack has been skillfully used. The best way to use the pack for this purpose I have discussed in the opening chapters of the book. Chances of attacking by the backs come either from the scrummages or from loose play. When a scrum is formed, it should be known to every one of the backs, even the full-back, what mode of attack is to be tried, *e.g.* going to the right, going to the left, short punt and follow up, a blind-side manoeuvre, a drop at goal, etc. It is only by knowing in advance that a player can be ready to do his best, whether it be by actual participation or by acting as a blind, with a view to putting the opposition off the scent. What actually will be the manoeuvre will depend upon a lot of circumstances. The part of the field in which the scrum takes place, the strength of your individual backs, the position taken up by your opponents, the strong points of your opponents, the state of the game, and the condition of the ground, are just a few factors that will govern a decision as to how to attack. These things are largely the concern of the captain of a side, but every member of the back division must apply his knowledge to the position as well, for, generally speaking, it is evident to every thinking member of a side what is the best plan to adopt, though the final decision, if there is any difference of opinion, will rest with the captain.

A fault one often sees with threequarters who are going to attack is that they stand too close up to the scrum. If it has been decided to try a passing movement, the threequarters on the side in which passing is going to take place should stand in echelon, very deeply. Let us put it the other way, for a moment, and suppose you stand close up to the scrum, and to the line running through the scrum from touch-line to line, and parallel to the goallines. As soon as you get the ball out, the defence closes up, and are on top of you before you have had time and room in which to manoeuvre. You want to get as far back as is reasonably consistent with giving you an opportunity to beat your opponents. You should never be afraid of this deep *échelon* formation. It gives you plenty of room and time in which to manoeuvre, it takes your opponents correspondingly longer to interfere with you, and it enables you to come up and take your pass at a great speed.

The Varsity match of 1920 will long be known as "Neser's match," so prominently did the South African, V. H. Neser, figure in it; but it was also a triumph for the deep *échelon* formation in attack. There was Neser well back from the scrum, and his "threes" equally well back from him. B. L. Jacot would never have scored his magnificent tries had he not had all that ground to cover before he got the final pass. It was that that gave him the momentum that enabled him to make what was ordinarily weak tackling look childish. Similarly, many a match has been lost because one side has been afraid to go deep enough from the scrummage, with the result that the attacks have been nipped in the bud every time. My advice to a side that is going to attack from a scrum is to stand deep, to decide what method you are going to adopt, and to let all your backs know without the opposition knowing if possible, and then to go into the movement with all the vigour you can command. If, on the other hand, you are out to check a back movement, you should be right level with the middle of the scrum, giving your opponents as little room as possible, so long as you are behind the ball.

It is always a great asset to a side to be able to start well. A lead quickly established is a lead likely to be added to, and correspondingly difficult to wrest from anyone. Players should have a run up and down the field before the actual kick-off, a few passing movements, and a kick or two, so that when the kick-off is taken they will be on their toes at once. If this is impracticable, they should handle the ball, if it is only in the dressing-room, and get the weight of it, have a sharp rub down, stretch their limbs, and generally get themselves looser and freer, as it were, so as to start the game seriously with the kick-off, and not five minutes af terwards. The classic illustration of the advantage of this, of course, is the 1910 England–Wales match, referred to earlier in the book, when a converted goal scored in the first minute gave us a moral and material ascendency that stood us in good stead all the first half and enabled us to add to the score during that half, and to win the match against a side that was probably better than ours.

If a player is cognisant of all that has been said about the position he plays in, and with the few ideas of combined play in this chapter, he should be able to take his place in the side, ready to do his individual work creditably, and to form an effective link with other men.

An aspect of team play that was for years neglected was the playing of the game in theory, – in the club-room. I know that a good deal of the success of West-country football between 1902 and 1912 was due to the serious attention that was given by the various clubs to informal talks one evening in the week. With a blackboard and some chalk, the various manoeuvres would be thoroughly discussed, and when anything new was to be tried, it was quite clearly demonstrated to everybody likely to participate in it, so that the theory was grasped before the practice was attempted.

Many an hour have I spent, with the various clubs I have been connected with, in this way. Some hard training, followed by one of these informal talks, was an ideal way to spend an evening, and not only was better play invariably the result, but a better spirit of *camaraderie* was obtained. I commend this practice to every club, as one likely to benefit it in every way. It has its funny side, too, for you will hear concocted the most weird football plots imaginable! You will always have your "theorist-gone-mad," with a scheme that would demoralise a couple of teams, let alone one! What does it matter if he is one of the poorest players in the side? It all helps to make the game interesting off the field as well as on it, and more than one brainy and practicable idea has been evolved by a man who was not fit to play for the side that has put it into practice. The time has gone when strength and physical fitness decided the issue. To-day it is the cleverer side that usually wins the match, so it is imperative that a team that hopes to do well should consist of men who put some thought into their play, as well as some vigour, and this cannot be done in a better way than by personal talks of the kind I have just described.

The best use to be made of a following wind is another matter that concerns the team as a whole, though it will be the captain who will give a general lead as to how this wind is to be used. Now a following wind can be a curse or a blessing, according to a side's ability to use it. It can be a blessing when there is a back or two able to judge accurately the strength and direction of the wind and to kick with the necessary strength and direction to enable the wind to be of the maximum assistance – a very difficult art, be it noted. The men who can do this will be able, when occasion demands it, to find touch well up the field, and a series of these kicks, with short sharp rushes following a line-out or a scrum, ought to lead to a score or two. Again, a well-judged punt can be very effective with a following wind, the forwards getting well under it to carry it on with a dribble or a bout of passing. A wind of this kind, too, may be used to advantage for drop-kicking or place-kicking, and, as I have said, it is an art that can be acquired by practice. A following wind can be a curse when players yield to the temptation to kick, and do so with poor judgment. The ball goes hurtling into touch, with little gain of ground, and takes minutes often to recover; whilst long punts up the field frequently result in the ball going dead and time being wasted, when a splendid chance of scoring had really presented itself. Again, with a strong wind it is impossible to pass properly or to dribble properly. In the former case, the ball naturally tends to go in front of the receiver, and even if the passer tries to allow for this by passing slightly into the wind, the receiver finds it difficult to take the ball satisfactorily. It is quite an accepted fact that passing movements are exceedingly difficult when a strong wind is blowing behind the side. The effect in dribbling is obvious, and very great judgment is necessary to keep the ball under control.

Playing against the wind has its double effect – one advantageous, the other the reverse. Needless to say, however well your man may kick, he cannot get the length into his kick that an equally skilful man can get from kicking with the wind. The best way to kick against a wind is by drop-kicking, giving the ball a low trajectory, or by punting in the same way. At all costs, the ball must be kept low, and I think this can be effected better with a drop-kick than with a punt. Passing is much more easily done against the wind. The pass should be thrown slightly more forward than usual, which really helps the receiver, for the ball comes back to him, as it were. Then dribbling is more easily done, too, as men can kick the ball harder with impunity, for the wind will pull it up, and enable it to be more easily kept under control.

Summed up, then, a wind blowing behind may be of great use if the kicking is carefully done, but for passing and dribbling it is bad, and in passing the players should keep closer together than usual to check the effect of the wind. Steady and sure kicking with forward rushes to follow should be the order of the day, especially if the backs have shown themselves to be powerless. With the wind against you, get plenty of drive behind your kicks, using a low trajectory and preferring the drop to the punt; but you will keep your kicking down as much as you can, for more success will probably follow sharp handling, the players keeping closer together than usual, and dribbling. What is more, if a player is forced to find touch against a wind, he had better not be too ambitious. It is far better to get the ball into touch ten yards ahead of you, than to attempt to gain thirty yards, see the ball blow into play, and have the chagrin of watching the other fellow, with the wind behind him, send the ball into touch fifty yards behind you. I would emphasise the value of every player trying to develop the team spirit. Let every man realise that, however well he plays, it is his side that benefits, and he will soon develop a keenness to make himself proficient for that purpose. The man who has the other conception, *viz*. that his own reputation is his main concern, is generally a nuisance to a side, though I am glad to say that in Rugby one rarely meets this sort of fellow, so essentially is the game one where a man may achieve little without the aid of someone else. A knowledge of the rules of the game, an acquaintance with the functions peculiar to his position, a realisation that he is a cog in a machine as a rule, but allowed to go on his own at times, and a keen sense of the honour of his side, are the main concerns of every member of a team.

12

Captaincy

It is extremely important to a side to be led well. This is a truism, but it is well worth repeating: a good team badly led may easily be beaten by a weak team well led. Besides, every member of a team enjoys his game more if he is led by a captain he admires or likes, or perhaps both admires and likes. It is a glorious feeling to play under a man who gets every ounce out of you because you love to please him, or because you know that his tactics are so brainily conceived that if you do your best your side will probably win.

Now let us consider the qualities that go to make up the ideal captain. Foremost among these qualities is that he shall be a born leader of men. What that phrase means exactly it is hard to define, but instinctively we all know the man in question. He is absolutely fair. The honest, hard-working forward who is a "trier" from beginning to end, but who rarely catches the eye, gets his word of praise as well as the flashy wing who is fortunate enough to score a number of tries. Every member of the side knows that in the eyes of his captain the sole criterion is "effort": the "slacker" alone is his *bête noir*. Again, he mixes with his fellow-players off the field in the same way, and spreads a spirit of *camaraderie* among them, he himself being the bond that unites them all. Above all, he is full of an infectious enthusiasm: he never spares himself, on the field or off, and the other members of the side get to copy him. During the match he is always ready to praise the good player, whilst the poor fellow who has made a mistake is censured in a congenial manner, a manner that conveys to the offender the fact that his error has been noticed, but that the captain is sure that it won't be repeated if possible. But if blame is necessary, this kind of captain is quite equal to it, generally wrapping it in a phrase or two, containing a few words, but all carefully chosen and very expressive! A man possessed of this temperament will make a splendid captain, even though he be quite an ordinary player, and have the crudest notions of tactics. In fact, the clubs that play the game not too seriously, just as a Saturday afternoon pastime, will find this is the ideal captain for them.

I remember having as captain of one of the most brilliant sides I ever played with, a man of this kind. He was easily the poorest player in the side, and one to whom the theory of the game meant little or nothing; but he led us magnificently. A word of praise from him gave us more pleasure than even a favourable Press notice, whilst slackness on our part was greeted with some good honest English, that was nothing if not to the point, and yet it left no sting. As far as the higher strategy of the game was concerned, he left that to his vice-captain and some of the cleverer members of the team, and this plan worked admirably. A man of this temperament, however, is one that is not always to be found, so we must consider the other qualifications in a captain, though always bearing in mind the fact that the temperament just described is the greatest asset any captain can possess.

A captain should be a sound tactician. All the modes of attack and defence he should be acquainted with, and he should carefully study the strengths and weaknesses of his own team and his opponents so as to know what tactics are likely to be most successful. Again, he must always think of his plan of campaign off the field, so that before the game commences he and his team know what manoeuvres they are going to carry out to begin with. But he must guard against the fatal tendency some captains have of being hide-bound to one scheme. The good tactician must be on the watch all the time, to see when a change of tactics is necessary, either to penetrate his opponents' defence or to beat off their attack, and he must be bold enough to make the necessary change even though it involves a risk. He will always be thinking out the game in theory, and will frequently call his side together and try over new tricks – in the club-room, then on the practice field, and ultimately in a match. All that I have said in the chapters on "The Team as a Whole" applies to the skipper more than to anybody else, for he is the "director" of all tactics practically, and the side will look to him for guidance in these matters.

Then it is also helpful if the captain is a good player, though I rate this much less highly than the other two qualities discussed. "Example is better than precept" is as true of Rugby as of other phases of life, and it certainly does buck a side up to see the captain perform brilliantly. Who that has seen the English captain, W. J. A. Davies, lead the Royal Navy can doubt this? Frequently one has seen a rather listless side wake up and do splendidly, just because Davies has electrified them by a glorious run or kick, and the other members feel that they ought to do something more worthy of such a captain. As a general rule, however, I have found that the most brilliant player is very rarely the best captain. Often he is made captain solely because of his individual brilliance, with the other two qualities either not possessed or only possessed to a slight degree. This is a great mistake. I should advise any club not to succumb to the glamour of a great player to make him captain. Any first-class footballer will give you numerous instances of sides that have done really badly because of the poor leadership of a brilliant player.

"What about the 'position' value of a player?" someone might ask. Well, whether a man be a forward, a threequarter, a half, or a full-back really does not matter very much. I have enumerated three qualities that might be looked for in a captain, *viz.* a gift of leadership, a knowledge of tactics, and great skill as a player. The former two are certainly more important than the position in which he plays; the third – well, it is perhaps of less value than the position the captain occupies.

The full-back position is in many ways a capital one from which to lead a side. This player, from his detached position, can see exactly how the various manoeuvres are faring, and wherein lie their weak points and their strong ones. He will thus know exactly how and when to modify the tactics of his side. By judicious kicking he can control the game of ten in such a way as to benefit his side's strong points, and weaken his opponents'. What is more, a player who is being watched from behind by a captain he admires very much, appreciates the word of praise he will get; whilst at the same time he will feel conscious that he is being carefully watched and will endeavour for that reason to do his utmost. Against the full-back, on the other hand, is the fact that he is comparatively a long way off, if a sudden change of tactics becomes necessary. Perhaps in the very middle of a movement a modification of it might become advisable. A captain in the heart of the movement itself could pass the word along quickly and quietly; the full-back would have to raise his voice, which would rob the change of its value, as the other side would probably hear him. Again, a "full-back" captain is very likely to find the strain more than he can stand, when he is called upon for strenuous defensive work all through a game. Under these circumstances he is almost bound to realise that any failure on his part will affect the morale of his side. Only the coolest and most capable of full-backs can stand this double strain without any detriment to their own play or their sides'. Still, I must confess that two of the ablest captains I ever saw were full-backs, *viz.* W. J. Bancroft, the captain of Wales for half a dozen years, and G. Romans, who captained Gloucester for some years. No move in the game escaped them, and they controlled the tactics of their side admirably. The man at the other end of the team, *i.e.* the forward, also has a lot to commend him for the captaincy. Endowed with the gifts of leadership, a forward should make a good captain. Were not John Daniell (England), V. H. Cartwright (England), Mark Morrison (Scotland), W. D. Doherty (Ireland); W. A. Millar and Paul Roos (South Africa), D. Gallaher (New Zealand), and W. J. Spiers (Devon), forwards? There have been few better captains than these. The main objection, nowadays, is that the game has become so open in its nature, and so much of it is confined to back play, that the "forward" captain is not always in a position to see what is going on outside the scrummage, and so cannot always modify the side's tactics to the best advantage. This can be overcome by having the vice-captain among the "outsides." It certainly stimulates the whole side to have a pack leader who is the embodiment of pluck and dash. If, then, there is a forward who can stir a side to doughty deeds by his enthusiasm and skilful leadership of the pack, by all means make him captain, choosing the cleverest tactician among the outsiders to be his "vice."

Two players whose positions, in my opinion, do not recommend them for the post of captain are the inside half and the wing threequarter. The former is too much in the thick of things to control his side properly. As a rule, he "can't see wood for trees," as far as manoeuvering by the threequarters is concerned, and I should be reluctant to appoint an inside half as captain. The opposite reason applies to the wing, *viz.* he is too detached from the play to be able to control it properly, and detached in a worse manner than the full-back, who, though equally far from the heart of things, is yet able to see them from the right angle, whereas the wing is not.

Outside half and centre threequarter are splendid positions from which to skipper a side, with my preference slightly for the latter. If you have a brilliant outside half who is inclined to go on his own too often, or to drop-kick too much, it is rather difficult to restrain him, should he be the captain. It is not impossible, of course, but he is much more easily checked if he can be talked to by one in greater authority than himself. A centre and a forward, then, are my choices for the posts of captain and vice-captain respectively, in that order, because of the predominance of open play nowadays.

Whilst a match is in progress a captain should be sparing in his advice to the other members of the side. The "fussy" captain is a nuisance, for all his good intentions. He is more of a hindrance than a help, if he is continually shouting "Do this!" or "Don't do that!" to the various players. He must be content to lay down general principles of tactics – and that largely off the field, – the details of which will be worked out by the individuals themselves far better if they are left on their own than if he "fathers" them all the time.

In recent years the "noisy" captain has become all too common. Meaning well, no doubt, he is yelling out some advice all the afternoon, and no player gets a chance of thinking for himself. I wonder the players don't openly resent it: I suppose they tolerate it because they realise that the player in question is doing it simply because he feels that that is the best way to help his side. Players certainly cannot like it, to be told what they are to do every time the ball approaches them, or to be censured openly for a mistake that was probably due to over-zealousness. No, the model captain for me is the man of few words, but when he does use any they are forceful and to the point, and they are uttered primarily for the player concerned, and not for the spectators; whilst for the rest he should inspire by example, and not by precept.

A word might here be said about the captain's part in the selection of the team. There was a time, in the early days of Rugby, when the captain picked the team on his own, and the practice still survives in the selection of the Varsity teams. But in this democratic age I suppose such an autocratic practice is more than most clubs can tolerate, and we have selection committees to do the work. One first-class club I know has a selection committee of nine! I would prefer the evils of selection by the captain himself, to those likely to accrue from selection by a committee of this size. Needless to say, every man's vote on this committee is of the same value, so that there are eight other members of that club who have as big a share in the choice of a team as the man who leads them. The whole thing is ridiculous.

Personally I think the ideal is for the captain to choose the team himself; for, if he had any sense, he would always find out from those whom he knew to be good judges what they thought of the various members of the side. If their opinions strongly clashed with his, he would pause before he made his final choice against their opinions, no doubt. But this procedure is not likely to be adopted nowadays, so one must be content with selection committees. The largest number I should have on a selection committee is five, but three would be preferable, and the captain should be the chairman. Obviously, a captain, elected with care, should have the most weight in the selection of his side, for he knows not only the respective merits of the men in question, but he also has a conception of the side as a whole, which will enable him to know how to fit in men so as to produce the best combination. This latter aspect is often forgotten, though a good captain always has it in mind.

There is one other aspect of a captain's duty that needs a few words. He will perhaps have to lead his side in a game where his opponents will adopt what he considers are foul tactics, and a difficult and thankless task will fall upon his shoulders. The weaker members of his side will be strongly inclined to retaliate (a perfectly human consequence, let it be confessed), for it is exasperating to be foully tripped, or charged, or tackled when not in possession. The strong referee will, of course, check this himself, but often the referee is unequal to the task, and the players get tempted to give "an eye for an eye and a tooth for a tooth." The captain will then have to restrain his men, realising that if he does encourage, or even tolerate, retaliation, it will be degrading to his side and to the game. He should be content with appealing to the referee, if he is convinced that the tactics in question are foul, and, if he cannot get assistance from that official, he must still endeavour to keep his men in hand. I know this savours of a counsel of perfection, but if any captain realises for a moment the other alternative, he will soon see that this piece of advice is the only right one. The other alternative is to let your men retaliate, and the thought of that being done systematically makes one shudder at the prospect. Again, a captain will occasionally have to play under a referee whose decisions are unsatisfactory, to say the least, and he will find a strong inclination on the part of his men (and on his own part, for that matter) to tell the referee what they think of him. Weak referees are like the poor, I am afraid – they are always with us, and must be tolerated. So it should be every captain's endeavour to keep his men from "letting off steam" at the referee. A quiet word from the captain may be effective in improving matters, but if it is not, and the referee goes on interpreting the rules in his own way-well, it must be so! Any captain who lets his team get out of hand under either of these circumstances, *viz.* foul tactics on the part of his opponents, or bad refereeing, has fallen short of the highest standards of captaincy. In this respect the ideal captain is the man who can control himself first and his team afterwards.

In addition to directing the tactics of the game, inspiring his men with his example, infecting them with his enthusiasm, and preventing them from getting out of hand, there are many small things that a captain has to attend to, all of which make for smoothness and efficiency in the working of a side. He should always have at least a couple of men whom he can call upon to take the placekicks. These men should be expected to make place-kicking a regular part of their training. With wet balls and dry ones, and from easy positions and hard ones, they should make themselves really proficient at this art. Then a couple of forwards, probably the flank men in the third row, should frequently train with the backs, not only to make them (the flank men) more capable of joining in the open play, but to enable them to take the place of any back who might happen to get injured. In fact, a captain should have a rough scheme whereby he could rearrange his team with comparatively little detriment to their play, if any member of the back division were hurt. It is also a captain's duty to see that his players attend to their boots, especially that they are properly barred or studded, and that the laces are sound (the value of this attention will be discussed in the next chapter).

A matter that will often need consideration from the captain is how best to take advantage of climatic conditions, notably wind and sun. With regard to the former, it is a safe principle to take advantage of a wind, if one wins the toss, mainly because it may drop later in the game. I have outlined how a following wind may be used to the best advantage in a former chapter, so will not do so again. But the captain will need all his power, even after he has decided that he will play with the wind, to see that due use is made of this advantage. Many and many a time have I seen captains allow this advantage to be of no avail, because they have not checked the injudicious kicking of their backs. I have heard people advocate a policy of playing against a gentle wind first half in the hope that it will be stronger in the second half. I would never risk it – the gifts the gods give should be taken at once: they are more likely to withdraw them than to add to them!

Then the sun can be an important factor. Everybody knows how very irritating and difficult it is to play with the sun low in the heavens, and dead in one's eyes. If a ground runs north and south there is, of course, nothing in it; each side will be similarly affected. On the other hand, if there is an east-to-west tendency, early in the season and very late in the season, it is often better to play against the sun when it has a fair altitude, *i.e.* first half, than later on in the afternoon, when it is lower and consequently a greater nuisance. This is often a contributory factor in enabling a captain to decide which way to play on a day in either of those parts of the year, when there is no wind, and there is a cloudless sky overhead.

Many other points will occur to captains when they bear in mind that, by all the means at their disposal, they must see that their men are fit and keen when they go on the field, that they must handle the team skilfully, and that, by occasional precept and continual example, they must get every ounce out of their men. Moreover, the fair name of any side is largely in the keeping of the captain, for not only is he responsible for the collective skill with which his team plays, but also for the spirit with which they play it, and, in Rugby, as in all forms of sport, a fair name is better than victory.

13
Training and Outfit

Much of the training necessary to enable one to play Rugby well has been dealt with in the chapters dealing with the various players, *viz.* forwards, halves, threequarters, and backs. Here I have in mind rather the kind of training players must indulge in, no matter what their positions are.

Every member should spend a part of his training time in learning to take and to give a pass, to field a ball cleanly, to kick well with one foot and not too badly with the other, and to dribble – that is obvious. There is not a single member of the team who can afford to neglect any of these arts. What is more, they can be learnt by practice, which cannot be said of all phases of Rugby tackling, for instance, of which more later. There was a time, as I have said in the section on "Forward Play," when it was not a serious matter if a forward could not give a pass properly, because handling was then looked upon as the concern almost entirely of an "outside," the forwards making up for this by greater proficiency with the feet. But with the development of the open game, it is a decided defect if a forward cannot handle the ball tolerably well. So all the team should go in for plenty of passing, remembering, amongst other things, that: –

1. A player must never slow up to give a pass.
2. A player must never slow up to take a pass.
3. It is nothing like such a bad fault to throw the ball too far in front of a man, as to throw it the slightest bit behind him.

The ideal pass is one that reaches the receiver in front of him, hip-high, and with plenty of pace.

Even the full-back must join in this, for the taking of passes helps him materially in his fielding of punts, whilst if he is proficient in giving passes, he is by that much the more able to start a bout of passing instead of kicking to touch.

With kicking, the degree of proficiency required varies considerably. As a rule, the full-back should be the best kick in the team, especially at punting. But every member of the side is bound to be so placed occasionally during a game as to cause a kick to be the best thing he can do. The forwards are the poorest kicks as a rule, which is only to be expected, but even they should be able to find touch accurately with one foot. As I write this, however, there comes to my mind a former magnificent English International forward, a member of my own club as a matter of fact, whose kicking was byword among us. He absolutely could not punt or drop-kick. As soon as he got the ball into his hands, any sort of kick was quite out of the question, and even in a serious match we have had to laugh at the grotesque attempt this player has made to punt. He was, however, possessed of such superb dash and was such a clever dribbler, that he was probably the best forward in England for one season. There is hope, then, for the forward who cannot kick, and, after all, it is better to be unable to kick and so be compelled to run, pass, or dribble, than to be "kicking mad" – not a rare disease nowadays. The drop-kick is more difficult than the punt, so a forward need not worry himself if he does not get very adept at it; but all the backs must give it serious attention. With regard to place-kicking, that is more difficult still, I think. I know I hated place-kicking, and was as big a "duffer" at it as the above-mentioned forward was at punting. Fortunately, however, you need never take a place-kick unless you want to. On the other hand, if a man finds that he can place-kick fairly well, he should certainly practise and make himself really good at it, for a reliable place-kick is a valuable asset to a side. On more than one occasion a forward has obtained his "Blue" simply because he was a better place-kick than another man, who was his equal in all other respects. One of our best sides scored III tries in the 1921–22 season, and only 37 of them were converted. That meant that 148 points were lost through faulty place-kicking, when a reasonably good kicker would have got at least a half of these. The team's training was not properly supervised, that is certain.

More than once in this book I have referred to the value of dribbling, and all I wish to do here is to emphasise the fact that dribbling should form an integral part of the training of every member of the side.

With regard to tackling, I am afraid that this art is best acquired by match practice. It is impossible to demonstrate in cold blood how to bring off a tackle. No player likes to be asked to dash along the field, and to allow himself to be tackled properly, *i.e.* vigorously, by someone else. One of two things happens. Either he shudders at the thought of a downright hard tackle as he approaches his would-be tackler, and eludes him; or he makes a poor attempt at a dash, preparing himself for the fall he knows he is going to get, and getting ready to take it in comfort! One can grip another player who is stationary or moving slowly, and show someone else where the arms should be locked, how the head should be placed, etc., but after that you must rely upon match practice. Even there, however, a practice match amongst one's own fellows is not very helpful, as men are not inclined to go all out in these games. Each man knows the other man's tricks, and tackling is thus made more easy. Again, tackling hard in practice matches is dangerous, in the way that having the gloves on with somebody "for a lark" is dangerous. Both forms of training need more control than are sometimes forthcoming. In no club that I have been concerned with have we tolerated serious tackling in practice: we have left the acquisition of this art to real matches. So, as far as tackling as a part of one's training goes, it is more the theoretical aspect of it that can be attended to than the actual practice. Tackling, passing, kicking, and dribbling (as distinct from kicking when one is in possession of the ball) form the foundations of Rugby, so that all should be practised diligently, the extra bit of practice being put into the different arts according to one's position.

In addition to this technical training, there is also the question of getting fit for a hard game, and maintaining that fitness. This is best done by a variety of ways. First, there must be plenty of running practice, whereby the ankles, knees, and hips are exercised freely, and the lungs trained to stand the strain. For all members of the team, steady long-distance runs are invaluable for "getting one's wind." Three or four times around the field at a steady jog-trot on the balls of the feet soon find out your condition. At first you are unable to do this distance –even once round makes you vomit and retch. Plenty of kicking about, hand-to-hand passing, and dribbling, however, all help, and gradually with this variety of training you soon find yourself able to increase the distance you can run in comfort. I am a great believer in this all-round training as a basis of getting fit. A capital modification of this long run is to practise short, sharp bursts during that run. They increase the strain for the time, which is helpful, and, better still, they prepare one to be quicker off the mark. Say the skipper is taking his side around the field. He tells them that a few times during the run he will shout "Go!" Then he wants every member of the party to go at top speed for about thirty yards, and at his next word of command to steady down to a jog-trot. It is also a fine thing to finish off a long run with an "all-out" dash of twenty or thirty yards. These bursts are splendid practice for enabling men to get off the mark quickly, and I think they are much more effective if done this way, than by practising standing starts.

Another form of training that is very beneficial is skipping. You need rubber shoes to do this best, certainly not studded boots, for skipping will have to be done on a hard surface. Steady skipping on the toes and balls of the feet improves your wind, makes you much more nippy on your feet, and is splendid for the shoulders, joints, and muscles. Often when it is dark and perhaps dangerous to do outdoor training, skipping is the only valuable mode of training practicable. I must say that I am not a very keen advocate of the use of mechanical contrivances in training, *viz.* dumb-bells, stretching apparatuses, etc. Fellows who like that sort of training probably benefit (by auto-suggestion, maybe) from a little, but these muscle-making exercises never appealed to me. To sum up these few hints on modes of training, then, I consider that: –

1. Kicking about carefully with a view to getting direction, and at times, in a sense, aimlessly, to develop the leg muscles,

2. Hand-to-hand passing,

3. Fielding practice,

4. Dribbling,

5. Skipping,

6. Running, to get one's wind, to increase one's speed, and to develop quickness off the mark; followed by a hot bath and then by a cold shower, should make any man fit to play Rugby, if, in addition, he leads a clean life.

I ought here to interpose a word on breathing. As everybody knows, the correct way to breathe is through the nose, both for inhalation and exhalation. In training it will be found of great assistance to practise this breathing through the nose. Skipping, for instance, is a splendid exercise to develop this habit, for it is steady and you can thus exercise your will power to keep to this nose-breathing.

How often do you see fellows running about the field with their mouths half-open, simply because they haven't trained themselves to base their breathing on nasal breathing. After very violent exercise you will find yourself naturally compelled to breathe through the mouth; but the more one has practised breathing through the nose, the rarer do those occasions for mouth-breathing become.

Generally speaking, most adult players find that intensive training during the first six weeks or two months of the season, say until the end of October, and an hour's practice of a lighter nature weekly after that, are enough to keep one fit for a match every Saturday afternoon. But, oh, those first six weeks! If all players feel as I did during that period, they must suffer. Every season I used to decide definitely that it would be my last, so much did I dread the preliminaries! And it was not that I did nothing in the summer, for I walked a good deal, played a little cricket, and also a little golf. Still, thank goodness, the glamour of the game, and the pleasure of the hot bath and cold shower, to say nothing of the brisk rub down that followed this agony, was too strong to let my weaker self win.

In the Provinces there is no difficulty about this kind of training, the early intensive kind or the subsequent steady kind, for the grounds and club-rooms are easily reached. Look at the splendid accommodation for players that is to be found in Bristol, Gloucester, and Leicester, to name a few that come to my mind. Very rarely, indeed, does a player find it impossible to get to his ground one night in the week, and have a run round and join in an informal talk afterwards. In London, though, it is different, and in most cases it is well-nigh impossible for men to get to their own club ground and indulge in any training. How the men manage to play as well as they do I often wonder, for in many cases, and those with tip-top clubs, one knows that the fellows have done no training since the previous

Saturday. Still, something should be done. Often there are gymnasiums or drill-halls in the neighbourhood of your residence where you can get in some skipping, or boxing, or ball-punching, or passing with a ball, or some such training, all of which stretch one's limbs and improve the "wind." One of the greatest forwards that ever played for England lived well away from any other players, and did all his training by running along the country roads at night. In this way he got wonderfully fit as far as wind and limbs were concerned, whilst his football genius enabled him to derive the maximum benefit from his Saturday games.

In schools and colleges, of course, there is no difficulty about the training. It is simply for the captain to consider it in all its aspects, and to draw up a definite scheme of training. For the rest, he has his players at hand. The greatest danger in this case is that of over-training, which every captain and player must guard against. The game is worth training for, and every player who possibly can manage it should get in some form of training, the ideal being to do it by daylight and on the field of play and with a ball. After one's school and college days that, I am afraid, becomes impossible, and then comes the test of one's enthusiasm, which always removes many otherwise insuperable obstacles.

Not much need be said about outfit. By far the most important part of one's outfit is the boots. They must fit perfectly, and it is always well worth the little extra expense to have them made to measure. They should be as comfortable as a well-fitting pair of gloves. It will be found that practically everybody likes to feel well-braced round the instep, and for that reason most players use very long laces to their boots, so that after the boots have been normally laced up, there is ample lace left to take a turn round the top of the boot, then a tight one round the instep (under the foot), and another turn to finish up with just above the ankle. Anything wrong with the lacing of a boot is a serious hindrance, detail though it seems. Even a trifle like the lace slipping over the top of the boot and getting on to your legs is enough to pull you up. You should strive to be carefully fitted for boots, and then to see that the laces are sound, and that the boots are fastened to your feet carefully and in the way suggested.

Which are better, bars or studs? This is largely a personal matter, but the weight of opinion is in favour of studs. I always felt more comfortable in them, I know that. Every player should see that his studs comply with the regulations (I fancy that not all players are aware that there are any regulations dealing with the nature of studs). More than one player has been badly injured by an illegal stud – one too long and pointed, as a rule, and sometimes, in addition, with an ugly nail projecting from the end. To be properly equipped one should have a couple of pairs of boots – one pair studded for the really soft grounds, and one for the harder grounds. Particularly long studs of ten hurt one's feet a good deal on a "bony" ground, whilst particularly short or flat ones are well-nigh useless on a muddy ground. The value of having boots studded to meet climatic conditions was strikingly illustrated when Cardiff met the famous South African team at Cardiff on January 1st, 1907. The night before the match it had rained in torrents, and there was little improvement on the morning of the match. Realising the value of sound studs, the Cardiff captain made it his business that Saturday morning to see that the boots of every member of his side were properly studded, the majority being re-studded for the occasion. The ground was like a quagmire, and Cardiff gave their opponents the heaviest defeat they sustained on their tour, partly because the South Africans were not used to such climatic conditions, but also because the Welshmen found their new studs decidedly useful!

One can easily be too careless about one's garters, and more than once have I seen a player seized with cramp in the calf, which has become chronic during the game, because he has worn garters that were too tight. Ordinary elastic garters of just the tightness that keeps the stockings up without causing any discomfort are the ideal.

Buckled belts should obviously be forbidden, though I have seen them used, whilst I also think that rings should not be worn by a player. I remember once seeing a man have a fearful gash on the eyebrow from an arm-swing – quite accidental – that caused the ring on his finger to strike the eyebrow. If only men thought of the accidental injuries that might arise from playing football with a ring on, they would not wear them. Certainly a captain should strongly advocate the removal of rings before going on the field.

With regard to shin-guards, forwards find them very useful, and they must save their shins a good deal. Some backs, even, wear them. I tried them once or twice, but on every occasion took them off before half-time, so much of a hindrance did I feel them. I played scrum half in first-class football for about twelve years, and did my fair share of rush-stopping and dribbling, I think, yet I cannot remember having any kicks on the legs that seriously inconvenienced me.

What a number of players one sees with knee-caps! They may be very helpful to fellows with weak knees – in fact they must be, – but surely there are not so many groggy knees about as all that. I feel tempted to think sometimes that fashion has a lot to do with this knee-cap wearing. The fellow who is fit and is prepared to take the risks that a game of Rugby entails, wants as little armour as possible, and what he does wear should be amply justified by an actual physical weakness, *e.g.* a really bad knee. Skull-caps, too, seem to appeal to some people, and not to others. Judging by the bad ears I have seen some forwards get, I should think some ear protection was necessary; but, again, the majority appear to do without them.

The main concern in one's outfit, then, is care of one's boots; the rest is all a matter of common sense and personal likes and dislikes, though I should like to emphasise once again the danger of wearing rings.

14

Refereeing

I wonder whether it is the same with referees as with poets – they are born, not made. It looks very much like it, for there is splendid machinery up and down the country for making them, and yet one sees a tremendous amount of bad refereeing in all parts. The various County Societies of Referees, and, above all, the London Society of Referees, are doing admirable work in organising the service of referees, in examining candidates, and in discussing knotty points and new regulations at their frequent meetings. Without the efforts of these Societies the game could not go on, for a system whereby the referee-choosing was done promiscuously could not be satisfactory. There are hundreds of clubs that play games every Saturday. All these matches have to be refereed, and it is only the unstinted labour of the secretaries of these societies that enables these games to be played as satisfactorily as they are. I say this because I feel that when people "grouse" at referees, they are apt to forget that even if they do happen to have to tolerate a bad referee occasionally, the system which enables such a man to get "on the list" is probably the best one that can be devised, and for clubs to be able to get a referee every Saturday without any bother is something to be profoundly thankful for. Let us realise this, then, whether we be dissatisfied players or dissatisfied spectators. Again, it is not a bad thing for developing one's sporting instinct to have, as referee, an A. O. Jones one week and an X. Y. Z. the next!

Let it be confessed, too, that the referee's lot is like that of Gilbert's policeman – not a happy one! An ill-controlled team can be very disturbing to the equanimity of the average referee. Sheer ignorance of the rules of the game is often responsible for this, and as a sensible referee is reluctant to send a man off the field for questioning his decisions, it is hard lines to have to put up with this sort of thing. And often, when it is not sheer ignorance, it is sheer cussedness! I will give an illustration of an experience I had myself, for I speak as one who has endured! I was refereeing a match in the West-country in 1919 between the Royal Naval College, Keyham, and another side – which I will not name (it was not a school side, I might say). Before the match both captains agreed that as the Cadets were very much lighter than their opponents, it would be better if we had none of the bullocking in the short lines that one often sees, and that the ball should be thrown in from touch with a pass of at least about three yards length and, where practicable, past the first player up. This, of course, was to prevent a big, hefty fellow from standing well back, working up a great charge, dashing up to take a pass practically out of the half's hands, and probably bowling over much too vigorously a very light player. Well, in the opposing team was a big forward who was easily the best player on the side. The first line-out that they had, he stood well back, timed his rush nicely, charged up the field, about a foot from the touch line, and shouted to the half for the ball. As this forward was "a man in authority" (a field-officer as a matter of fact), he was given the ball. I blew the whistle, and asked for another throw-in, on the ground that both captains had agreed that they would not indulge in this manoeuvre. The forward in question was furious; he had never heard of such a thing: had I ever seen a game of football? etc., etc. The captain of the side, a humble individual off the field compared with the forward in question, was well-nigh powerless, and the first half of the game was completely spoilt. I called the player back every time he did it, and he became more and more furious until, when I ventured to pacify him (for I did not want to send him off, knowing his position) by what I thought was a sane remark, he wound up a fierce diatribe with: "Don't talk to me! I've played more football than you've ever seen! At half time some naval friends of mine who had accompanied the Cadets had a word or two with him, telling him, amongst other things, that I had played a little football myself; and in the second half he was silent, though sullen. But he took part in no more lines-out. I only mention this to show that I am well aware of the difficulties of refereeing, for I don't know what would have happened, in the match I have described, to a poor referee who had no name to support him. I can imagine this particular forward barging up to a line-out and hurling the referee off the field as well!

It is obvious, then, that to be a good referee one must have the right temperament – a compound of good humour, sympathy, and strength of character. He must not be perturbed by the open grumbling of a player or two, or by the sullen "grousing" that is equally annoying. A smile, and at the same time a strict adherence to one's decisions, will generally cause a grumbler to realise that he had better make the best of the refereeing, whatever he thinks of it, for it will go on as it has done; whilst he will soon realise that a continuance of this interference with the referee – for it *is* interference – may lead to "marching orders." Sympathy, too, is needed. An occasional explanation of a ruling that seems to puzzle a team is very helpful, and will often prevent a side from becoming unsporting. Strength of character is equally essential, if not more so. Unless you are able to withstand the protests of a body of players, and to adhere to a decision that you have once given, you had better be content with letting others do the refereeing. The painful refereeing I have seen, of men who have tried to please first one team, then the other, and the crowd all the time! Certain referees get a reputation for their weakness in this way, and unscrupulous players don't hesitate to appeal furiously for knocks-on, off side, obstruction, etc., because they know that the referee is prone to respond to their vocal efforts, whether the decision is right or not. If a maxim were needed for this aspect of refereeing, it might be: "My decision, right or wrong!" The strongest referee will sometimes have to modify a decision, but this had better be a very rare occurrence. A man knows when he has given a decision that is manifestly unfair, and if he realises his mistake in time, he should alter it at once. The worst thing he can do is to let himself fall into a system of "compensatory" refereeing, whereby he lets "A" have the benefit now, "B" then, and so on. If a bad decision has been given, and it is too late to alter it, forget all about it, and go on being firm. More than usual firmness is often necessary in dealing with well-known players, and I have met many such players who have been a perfect nuisance with their bickering at the referee all the time. A vein of humour, sympathy, and firmness, then, are temperamental qualities a referee should strive to cultivate, if he is not endowed with them naturally.

A good knowledge of the rules he must have, of course. But this is a source of great danger to referees, and here I must cross swords for a moment with these excellent Referees' Societies I have alluded to. It is possible to be an absolute authority on the rules, to know them from the first word to the last, large print and small, and yet to be a hopeless referee; and I am afraid that this is due in part to the nature of the referees' meetings one attends or reads about. Every detail is thrashed out with meticulous care, and men gloat over knotty points for hours, forgetful of the fact that this is a game for men in the prime of life, who will play it with great vigour, and that the spirit must be considered as well as the letter. Technical infringements of a quite unimportant nature will be met with that must be overlooked, or the game will be ruined. Anyone can call to mind the many occasions when the main feature of a match has been the incessant blowing of the whistle, the referee continually pulling the game up for these petty infringements that are committed accidentally by both sides, and that quite counterbalance themselves. The theory of the game thus tends to become divorced from the practice. By all means let us discuss the rules, and try to get at the spirit behind the rule, so as to obtain a uniform and satisfactory method of interpreting this rule. At the same time, however, let us always realise that a knowledge of the rules is only one of the many qualifications, and that equally important is a careful study of the practice of the game. I would advise every person who thinks he has the temperament to referee creditably, to study the rules first, to play some football himself, to watch many games to see how the rules are interpreted and what sorts of infringements should be allowed to pass as they are made by both sides, and then to try a little active refereeing, interspersing it with more watching. Above all, don't be deluded into a false opinion of your refereeing ability by the fact that you cannot be caught by any question dealing with the laws of the game. Your opinion may receive a rude shock if you are asked to referee a keen "local" match one day! I hope I shall not be misunderstood. I realise that the rules and their interpretation must be carefully discussed from time to time; but this theoretical aspect should not be allowed to overshadow the practice of the game. It is because I think that some of the bad refereeing, by excellent fellows in all parts of the country, many of them great friends of mine, is due to this tendency that I have given the matter such prominence.

It was my good fortune to play under my old friend, the late A. O. Jones, scores of times. He was an ideal referee, possessing all the qualities I have enumerated. On the other hand, you never saw "Jonah" poring over rules, or setting himself, or anybody else, Rugby "puzzles." In fact, I will go so far as to say that he would have probably failed had he been examined by an official keen on the *ipsissima verba*. But nobody would have failed him, after seeing him referee a game. Still, I don't want to imply that the race of referees died out with A. O. Jones. There are still some excellent ones about. One piece of refereeing I saw at Twickenham last season, in a club game, was as good as anything I have ever seen. My complaint is that there are not so many really good referees as there ought to be, and I give my conception of what qualifications a referee should have, and of what referee societies should avoid, in the hope that "referee-appointing" bodies may, if they think these ideas are worthy of it, give them a little thought.

I will end this chapter as I began it: the best referees are born, not made. In spite of that, though, here are a few words of advice that may help a budding referee: know your rules; watch many games to see how these rules are interpreted; try to be cheery and sympathetic, but yet firm; be consistent (a great point this); and, last but not least, have a whistle that can be heard, not one that sounds as though it came out of the Christmas bran-tub.

15
The Spirit of the Game

I suppose every game has its "spirit," though what that actually means it is difficult to say. Still, we should all be able to recognise its absence or presence in any player or team, though we could not define it. There are certain manifestations that enable us to form our opinion, and much as I realise the task I am undertaking, yet I feel that in a book on the playing of Rugby something should be said whereby player and spectator alike might be helped in the forming of a judgment as to whether certain tactics are evidence of the right spirit of the game, or the opposite. This spirit of Rugby is the result of tradition, and with all the changes that modern conditions bring about in the actual playing and conduct of the game, it is more than ever necessary that the essence of the game shall remain the same, and that "playing the game," whether the side is losing or winning, is the sole basis for calling the players true Rugby men.

Let us consider, first of all, a few instances of practices frequently met with to-day, that are not in accord with the spirit of the game. (I hate this negative method of explaining the spirit of the game, but certain advantages accrue to it.) It is no uncommon sight to see a side take advantage of the weakness or ignorance of a referee. The men realise his shortcomings and play accordingly, modifying their tactics to suit those conditions. Putting the ball into the scrummage unfairly, getting offside on the blind side of the referee, charging in the line-out when the referee cannot see the action – these are just a few of the things that, I am sorry to say, we see all too often. The idea seems to be that all is fair that escapes the referee – a wretched principle, everyone must admit. But unless captains are clearly of opinion that this is wrong, and that they will insist upon every member of their side playing the game as it should be played, regardless of the referee's shortcomings, we shall continue to meet with this unsportsman-like play. The rules of the game are definite enough; if they are violated, whether the referee sees the infringement or not, it is not fair and square Rugby. I strongly advise all schools and colleges in particular to root out this tendency (if it exists), for it is more easily rooted out there than elsewhere, as the conditions are generally so much more favourable. Then, as youths matured in this kind of Rugby join other clubs up and down the country, they will tend to leaven a whole that might have been inclined to be unfair in the way I have mentioned.

Another failing one comes across sometimes is of a different nature. A side that plays hard Rugby, with plenty of enthusiasm and vigour, but little skill, especially combined skill, is nearly always beaten by a side possessing the same qualities to a slightly less extent, but possessing, in addition, great combined skill. The latter side has given the theoretical side of Rugby a good deal of thought, and is able to work out on the field manoeuvres that their opponents have never seen or heard of. There is a marked tendency under certain circumstances for the winning team to be accused by their opponents of playing unfairly. This is not in accord with the spirit of the game, I am sure. Rugby football at its best is a combination of vigour and cleverness. An undue attention to the former, with a comparative disregard of the latter, does not lead to the highest standard of Rugby. Consequently, when a side is beaten by a cleverer side, it should be very chary about calling its conquerors "shady." For years, the very word "tactics" connoted something bad – not honest Rugby. This was, in part, deserved, because for a very long time there were quite a number of clubs that seemed to give a tremendous amount of thought to the working out of manoeuvres that were fair in a sense, but were hardly in the spirit of the game. I won't go into details; let it suffice to say that clubs did earn this reputation. But, as always, the pendulum swung to the other extreme, and a clever side all too often was dubbed "shady" when it was simply honestly clever. The moral of it all is this: a club should hesitate to brand another one as unsporting. Let any player ask himself whether the action in question is first fair, *i.e.* whether it conforms to the rules of the game, and then let the player in question make quite sure that neither he nor any member of his side is prone to adopt the same tactics under the same conditions, or would if he could. I attach great importance to this latter aspect of it, for there is any amount of cant and humbug among players themselves and among clubs. There is no room for can't in a game like Rugby.

I will give just one specific case. A player about to kick-off after a score, has the bulk of his players on one side of him, as though he is going to give the usual kick that the majority on that side of him can follow up. Just before he actually kicks, however, he arranges with a fast forward to keep on his other side, ready for a short kick in the latter direction. The kick-off is taken, and the ball is sent to the side opposite to where the majority of the players are. The ball is fielded by the forward who has been told of the trick, and quite a lot of ground is gained because his opponents are marking the other forwards. Sharp practice? Certainly not; it is absolutely fair and honest, and only requires watchfulness on the part of the opposition to make the manoeuvre of no avail. Surely, then, if it is fair and done in the open, there can be nothing wrong with it. Yet I have heard players who have done this trick successfully classed as "unsporting," although I have seen it practised by every kind of club, including Varsities, Counties, and International sides.

Again, one occasionally hears a manoeuvre dubbed as "shady" if done by a certain type of club, but allowed to pass by other clubs. This cannot be too strongly condemned. Foul play is foul play, whoever is responsible for it, and I feel that a lot of things are tolerated in sides which should know better, because this discrimination is made. The crowds that frequent our matches are partly responsible for this, by the blind, and oft-times ignorant, enthusiasm they work up for the home team, and I realise that it needs a firm executive and high-minded players to resist the temptation begotten of an enthusiastic following. But this firmness must be forthcoming. In running a school team, I should advise coaches to err on the other side, and to exact a higher standard of fairness from their own team, if possible, than from their opponents. It is because I have so often seen the same tactics cheered by a home crowd when carried out by a home player, and hooted when done by a visitor, that I write so strongly.

Here is an illustration of what I mean. It is absolutely unfair to tackle a man who is not in possession of the ball. There is a little excuse, sometimes, if the man you have tackled seemed certain to get the ball, just before you tackled him, only the would-be passer feinted instead. Otherwise, of course, there is no excuse. Not long ago, when watching one of the best teams in the country, I saw the home full-back deliberately bring down an opponent, who had cleverly kicked over the farmer's head and would have scored had he not thus been unfairly tackled. There was no justification whatever, for the kick had been completed yards before the full-back reached his man. The referee was weak, and a touch-down, instead of a penalty try, was the result. Some of the crowd laughed, some cheered, nobody hooted. I was on the same ground some weeks later, and a visitor brought off the same unfair tackle. You should have heard the yells of the crowd!

It is surely very unsporting to gloat over a beaten man or side. I was never more ashamed of myself than on one occasion many years ago. The side I was connected with was a splendid one, and among our threequarters was a very clever side-stepper. The Old Merchant Taylors, always. a most sporting team, were our opponents, and their skipper was the late John Raphael, a great sportsman, and one of the many who gave their lives for the country in the War. The back I have referred to got possession on one occasion, near the grand stand, with Raphael near him. By dodging and side-stepping our back beat Raphael half a dozen times very cleverly, all in the space of about twenty yards. The crowd shrieked with laughter. Finally, Raphael made a leap at the elusive figure of his opponent, just as the latter was punting to touch, and went full length on the ground. Needless to say, the "gallery" enjoyed it immensely, but when our threequarter turned round and grinned with a sort of contempt at Raphael as he lay prone – well, I wished I could sink into the earth. For a chivalrous opponent, which John always was, to be treated in this unsporting way almost made my blood boil.

I won't multiply these illustrations of what do not constitute the "spirit" of the game, for, as I have said, I hate this principle of preaching good by talking about evil. But these unsporting practices are so frequently met with nowadays that I feel constrained to mention them, so as to warn young players against them when they see them, for they are not in the true succession of Rugby.

Now a word or two on the positive side. The rules of the game are fixed. One sure way to play the game in the right spirit, obviously, is to adhere to those rules. This implies a knowledge of them, which precious few players really have. In fact, more than a few of the unsporting tactics, and allegations of unfairness on the part of the other side, are due to this ignorance of the rules. It is possible, I know, to be really sporting in one's game, and yet be ignorant of the finer points of the rules. But it is far easier to earn the reputation of being fair, if one knows the rules. One can, then, at any rate recognise right from wrong, whatever one's nature is – I mean, naturally sporting or otherwise. Every captain might very well take the rules of the game through with his men at a few informal talks. Mind, I don't want to imply that a knowledge of the rules leads necessarily to a possession of the spirit of the game. It often does not, but it is of great assistance.

After that, the true Rugby man is whole-hearted, and is prepared to take risks. It is invidious to make comparisons, but I do say that there is no team game where a man can display such abandon as in Rugby. What more do you want than to be in possession of the ball twenty yards from the line, and to know that if you put all your vigour into your run and dash for the line, you will benefit not yourself so much as your side! You do not say to yourself: "I might score here if I go on, but I fancy the opposition is too strong, so I will wait for a better opportunity". No, you risk it, and make the attempt. That is another manifestation of the spirit of the game, then, the glorious love of adventure, as seen in the individual and collective dashes against heavy odds.

To take whatever luck you get, good or bad, and to make the best of it, is another obvious sign of the spirit of the game. For that reason, I dislike the practice creeping in now under certain circumstances, of letting another man take the place of an injured one. It is very creditable to the side that makes the suggestion, but the offer should be always graciously but firmly refused. (Needless to say, I am not referring to some Trial games, where changes are made, injuries or no injuries.) That is one of the glorious aspects

A FREE KICK

of the game, where you steel yourself to fight your hardest whatever good luck your opponents have, and whatever bad luck your side gets. I can't resist the temptation to quote a line of Virgil that I have often thought of when in a tight corner-on the field and off: –

Tu ne cede malis, sed contra audentior ito.

That is the spirit, then. A team that is keen, clean, and determined, even though it is being soundly thrashed, is doing the game and itself good. In fact, the true spirit of the game is generally more easily displayed in adversity than in prosperity, as it were.

Sometimes one sees stronger and cleverer men take an unfair advantage of lighter and less clever men, and treat them with a certain amount of thoughtlessness. I have even seen school teams badly mauled about by big fellows who simply revelled in their physical superiority. This is contemptible, and, because it is met with, I strongly advise masters in charge of school sides to be careful about pitting boys against adults. Sometimes it is good for the boys to see what adults can do. In fact, it is not a bad thing in their days, when boys are inclined to believe that they know all there is to know about a game, to give them proof positive that they still have a lot to learn. But masters should make quite sure of the team they are inviting. It is far better to let boys go to Varsity and International matches to see the higher standards of play, than to run the risk mentioned.

The best way to develop the right spirit in a team is for that team to be in charge of a good coach. If you have the right man, you will see at once what it is to be a player of the right spirit. Enthusiasm and fairness ooze out of this man, and boys especially, unconsciously, copy him in all his ways. The Rugby coach at school has a glorious opportunity. He is not only teaching boys how to play a certain game, but he is all the time training them in habits of chivalry, honesty, and the vigorous but clean use of bodily strength. This "spirit" is so potent that we recognise it in a school team at once, and we know that either I the coach or the skipper is infusing into his men, more by example than precept, as a rule, the spirit of the game. As I have said, with schools this is done by the coaches. What the War has meant to us in this respect! Rugby men by the thousands gave their lives freely, in the very spirit that we are talking about, and their places cannot adequately be filled for some time yet. In clubs for adults, sometimes a keen old player takes an interest in the men and infuses the right spirit, but generally the duty devolves on the captain. Whoever it is to whom the members of a side look up, that person must always bear in mind what I said at the end of the chapter on Captaincy, *viz.* a fair name is better then victory.

Rugby is a game of hard knocks, a game for strong, healthy men. If these hard knocks are given and taken in the right spirit, one side will bear no ill-will towards the other, but will strive with all its might to beat its opponents, and afterwards both will look back upon the game as something that has given them great pleasure, whatever the result.

16

Looking Ahead

Never was there so much Rugby played as at present. Public Schools and Colleges that have never before played the game officially have now taken to the game by the dozens, whilst up and down the country old clubs that had become defunct have been revived and have called into being once more the pleasantest of recollections; whilst in every kind of district – rural, industrial, commercial, residential, etc. – crowds of new clubs have sprung into being. Less important, but interesting in itself, is the fact that the followers of the game have increased enormously in number, as the crowds at Twickenham, Bristol, Birmingham, and Leicester, to name but a few centres, amply prove. The only pity is that the difficulty of finding playing pitches makes it inevitable that among the crowds one sees at Rugby games there are so many young men who ought to be playing the game instead of watching it. The game cannot be doing its maximum good when fellows who would like to be playing have to be satisfied with watching. This "ground" difficulty is a very serious hindrance in populous areas to the development of the game – and every other game for that matter. What a blessing it would be if some concerted action, be it parliamentary or municipal, could be taken to help to provide adequate playing pitches for our more vigorous games, among which Rugby takes an honoured place! The nation would be all the better for it, if healthy young fellows could look forward to the winter Saturday afternoons as occasions when they could indulge in a game themselves, however indifferently they played it. I feel quite confident that much of our present unrest would disappear if the healthy and spirited young men of to-day regularly engaged in an honest and vigorous sport, where they could work off some of their excessive energy, mental and physical. In connection with this "ground" difficulty, the Rugby Union might do a little more than it has done. True, it has given generous financial aid to some clubs since the War, but there is still room for improvement. After the payment of debts and careful provision for the future, almost the first claim on the Rugby Union funds should be for grants towards helping clubs to rent or purchase grounds, so that they might start to play. It is this initial ground expense, even where a ground can be found, that deters many a body of enthusiasts from forming a club. If the various County Unions and the Rugby Union itself give this matter careful and regular attention – and the parent body can do most, acting through its County representatives – we shall have fewer of these healthy young men watching Rugby instead of playing it.

I am afraid, however, that there is another reason why one sees so many youngsters at matches nowadays – a reason that is not quite so satisfactory as the one just mentioned. Many fellows there are who are prone to resign from a club if they cannot find a place in the First or "A" team: if they are picked for a side other than those two they seem unable to find much pleasure in playing, and prefer to become spectators. This is strongly to be deprecated. I am a great believer in hero-worship, and have indulged in a good deal of it myself – and do now! To watch men like W. J. A. Davies, C. A. Kershaw, C. N. Lowe, H. H. Forsayth, or W. W. Wakefield, to name only a few brilliant players of to-day, is bound to engender a sort of hero-worship in a youngster (if it doesn't, I am sorry for him!). But it is wrong to forsake participation in the game for hero-worship only. Combine them: have your games with your club, and also find opportunities, if convenient, to go and see these men who represent the game at its highest and best. My advice, then, to any young fellow is to join a Rugby club if he can, and to play as well as he can. It matters not whether he is in the "Firsts" or "C" team – the game is the main thing. Ask any member of the weakest sides turned out by clubs like Rosslyn Park, or the Wasps, or the Old Blues, that run about half a dozen sides every week, whether he enjoys his games. You will generally find that he has "loved" it, even though he is a very incapable player, judged by the cold light of efficiency. Mind, one does not want to be hypocritical about this. It is only human to prefer playing for the "A" team to playing for the "E" team; but if natural disability or the exigencies of one's work make great skill impossible of attainment, get the best you can – and there is a tremendous lot to be got – out of the class of football you are in. For this reason, it behoves clubs that exist for the sake of giving men opportunities to play Rugby, rather than to produce "red-hot" sides, to make the best provision they can for every one of the sides they turn out. Fortunately, there are very many clubs in London and in the Provinces that do this splendidly, and at some of the annual functions of these clubs, I admire tremendously the keen fellows present, the bulk of whom have had a most enjoyable season, with an utter disregard for crowds, Press comments, etc., that attend the doings of first class teams. We do want to see fewer young players who are physically fit attending Rugby matches regularly. By all means let them pay due homage to the heroes of the game; but let that be occasional, not regular.

The increasing support that clubs are getting is a source of danger to the game – paradoxical though it may seem. The troubles of amateur sport begin when "gates" are taken. A charge for admission implies an obligation to the public, and committees are often torn between their duty to the public and their duty to the players. Without a doubt, the latter is the more important, and I feel that consideration for them is not quite so strong as it should be, when I see fixture lists annually increasing in length. Within the last twenty years many clubs have increased their lists by about half a dozen matches – and this at a time when the game has become much faster than it used to be! I know the difficulties of club executives, as I was for many years connected with two of the leading provincial sides; rival attractions and the demands of the supporters are hard to fight against. Still, the fight should be made, and the fixture lists brought back to a maximum of about thirty-six games, when players could maintain their fitness and their enthusiasm all through the season (I cannot imagine many players who started early in September enjoying the matches at the end of April), whilst their occupations would be less interfered with-an important aspect of the matter.

On the whole, the game of Rugby is well organised, and there is little fault to find with its administration – this savours of "damning with faint praise," which is far from my intention, so I will go further and say that the game is well administered. The parent body is naturally a slow-moving one, and there are occasions when I feel profoundly thankful that it is so. From time to time one hears the most weird and fantastic suggestions made for the so-called "improvement" of the game, and a too-responsive body might be led to adopt some of these suggestions before fully realising what they involved. Some of the laws of the game are absurdly illogical, for example, but it seems to me that their very "illogicalness" is one cause of the "Rugby spirit" that we all feel so proud of, and I should be sorry to see the rules so recast as to clear away all these "defects" (as some people call them). To my mind, a rule should only be tampered with when the traditional interpretation of it seems to be more honoured in the breach than in the observance, or when there are so many interpretations of it that categorical restatement is necessary. Again, if bad practices creep into the game, it is not sound policy to rush to formulate a new rule by which those practices may be eliminated. It is far better to wait until a continuance of this evil makes it certain that the spirit of the game is unable to cope with the nuisance. Then, if the game is undoubtedly degraded by these practices, they must be "ruled out." But one must never forget that in every game an increase in the number of rules means a reduction in the scope for developing the spirit of the game.

The Rugby Union should, in my opinion, do more to encourage the County Championship, especially by consultation with the metropolitan counties. Club, county, and country are the natural grades in the game, and every one should feel it an honour to progress from one step to another. Needless to say, he does do so when it is to the last stage, and he does in all parts of the country outside the metropolitan area when he advances from club to county. In the North and the West, county football is the height of the average player's ambition, for he realises that he will need either genius or luck, or a little of both, to enable him to obtain the highest honours. And the spectators view these county games in the same light. Who that has been there can forget the excitement of a county match at Redruth, Exeter, Brigdewater, Gloucester, Hartlepool, Headingley, or Aigburth? County football, however, loses a lot of its value by the fact that all the counties do not take it with equal seriousness. I know the very great difficulties in the London area – qualification, interference with club matches, etc., but I am confident that if a solution were honestly sought it could be found – or a much better arrangement come to than exists at present. As I said to begin with, the Rugby Union cannot do much itself, but if the counties concerned were aware that the parent body was extremely anxious that county football throughout the country should be put on a better footing, they would probably be ready to bring things into line.

I am delighted to see that the old Champion County *v*. The Rest fixture is to be revived. For years it provided a splendid game, and from a "Trial" point of view was often very valuable. What is more, it is another recognition of the existence of the County Championship Competition. Some would wish this match to figure at the end of the season, as a sort of "test. But there is a lot to be said against it. By the time the Championship is settled, many players are feeling stale, for the best players begin to get slack after the Scottish match, and there probably would not be that individual brilliance in the Rest team that would counteract the better combination of the champions. I can well imagine the feelings of the Champion County, though, and its supporters, animated of ten by a desire to show how many more players from that county should have played for their country! The best solution is the one to which we are likely to return, *viz*. that the Champion County of one season should play, early in the next season, the best team drawn from the Rest, and that this match should be looked upon as a preliminary "Trial" game.

A splendid feature of the season 1921–22 was the number of club histories that were produced. It really made capital reading to dive into the past, and see how those fine old fellows gloried in a game, which, in its early stages at least, demanded more energy of body than of mind. What did they care about crowds or comments? It is invidious to single out any particular volume, but the "humanness" of the History of the Clifton Club appealed to me immensely. We are now getting quite a body of "Rugby Literature," and when we see one of the ablest of our younger poets and critics, *viz*. J. C. Squire, making a Rugger match the theme of one of his longer poems, we begin to realise that we shall have to find a niche in our bookshelves for serious "Rugby Literature," as cricket enthusiasts have been able to do for a long time for "Cricket Literature."

In this connection, isn't it time that a sequel were written to the Rev. F. Marshall's classic "Football: The Rugby Union Game"? Everybody would welcome a volume dealing with the development of the game from the time that Marshall's book leaves off (1891), either to 1914 – the "War" break – or to last season, the fiftieth anniversary of the founding of the Rugby Union.

The 1922–23 season is the centenary of the occasion when William Webb Ellis "first took the ball in his own arm and ran with it, thus originating the distinctive feature of the Rugby game, A.D. 1823," as the inscription on the mural tablet at Rugby School has it. This is a fitting occasion, then, for the Rugby Union to "father" the sequel to Marshall's book, for there were giants in the days between 1891 and 1921, of whom we should possess a worthy record.

Nearly all the signs are auspicious: clubs are more numerous, crowds are larger; the game is being played by increasing numbers of Public Schools and Colleges; the Press is giving more prominence to the game than ever; and the play, though hardly so clever as it was before the War, is, I think, cleaner. With a steady supreme authority, by which I mean one that will move with the times, but will never forget the traditions of the game it watches over, careful club-control, and a continuance of the individual enthusiasm that exists at present, we can have no misgivings for the future of Rugby football.

APPENDICES

Bye-Laws of the Rugby Football Union, Etc.

As passed at the General Meeting held on September 20, 1893, and Amended, 1894–5–6.

1. The name of the society shall be "The Rugby Football Union," and only clubs entirely composed of amateurs shall be eligible for membership; and its head-quarters shall be in London, where all general meetings shall be held.

2. The committee, who shall be elected annually, shall consist of the five following officers, namely, – a president, two vice-presidents, an hon. secretary, and an hon. treasurer, and sixteen other members. All past presidents of the Union, who shall have attended two regularly convened committee meetings during the previous year, shall be members of the committee. Seven shall form a quorum; the chairman shall have a casting vote in addition to his first vote. No past president shall be entitled to vote on the selection of teams unless he has been chosen to act on the sub-committee elected for that purpose. Any vacancy in the committee occurring during the year shall be filled up by the committee.

3. All clubs being members of the Rugby Union in the following districts shall have the following representation on the committee, and may elect the number of representatives on the committee respectively placed opposite their names, namely: –

Cambridge University	One
Cheshire	One
Cumberland and Westmoreland	One
Durham	One
Lancashire	Three
London District	Four
Midland Counties	One
Northumberland	One
Oxford University	One
South-Western District	Two
Yorkshire	Four
Total	Twenty

The South-Western district shall comprise the counties of Cornwall, Devon, Gloucester, and Somerset, and the London district all clubs and counties not included in any of the above. All such elections shall be in the hands of the hon. secretary by August 7; if not, the new committee shall fill up any vacancies.

The manner in which the above twenty seats are distributed may be altered at any annual general meeting, on the vote of the majority of those present, provided notice of such proposed alteration be given to the hon. secretary not later than August 7.

4. There shall be sent to each club, not later than August 14 in each year, a list of the twenty representatives so elected, together with the committee's nominations of

officers for the ensuing year, namely, a president and two vice-presidents, nominated from the above twenty representatives; an hon. secretary, not necessarily from the above twenty; and an hon. treasurer, nominated either from the above twenty, or from the past presidents. Any club has the right to make further nomination of officers only, but any for president or vice-president must be from the twenty elected representatives, for treasurer from the above twenty or from past presidents; any such nominations must reach the hon. secretary by August 21, and a complete list of all nominations must be sent to each club with the circular calling the annual general meeting.

5. The election of officers shall take place at each annual general meeting, and shall be decided by a majority of those voting. In case the hon. secretary be elected from the twenty elected representatives, then such representation shall become void, and the county, university, or district shall elect another representative to fill such vacancy. In case a district has to make another election, such must be done within fourteen days of the annual general meeting; if not so made, the Committee shall fill the vacancy.

6. Any club willing to conform to the Rules of the Union shall be eligible for membership, but before being admitted, such club must be duly proposed and seconded by two clubs belonging to the Union.

7. That the annual subscription, payable in advance, of each club belonging to the Union, be £1 1s, with an entrance fee of 10s 6d, payable on admission. The annual subscriptions of all clubs shall fall due in September. Any club whose subscription has not been paid before March 1 shall be struck off the Union list.

PLAN OF THE FIELD.

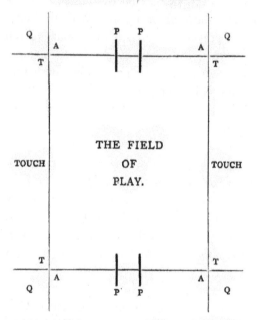

AA, AA.—Goal-lines.   TT, TT.—Touch-lines.

PP, PP.—Goal-posts.   QQ, QQ.—Touch in Goal.

The touch-lines and goal-lines should be cut out of the turf, or otherwise well defined.

The field of play should not exceed 110 yards in length, nor 75 yards in breadth, and should be as near those dimensions as practicable.

The maximum extent of the dead-ball line is 25 yards.

The posts and flags marking the centre and 25 yards lines should be kept well back from the touch-lines.

8. The annual general meeting shall be held in September in each year for the election of officers, the consideration of the bye-laws, laws of the game, and rules as to professionalism, and other business.

9. Each club shall be entitled to send one representative only to any annual or special general meeting, exclusive of the officers and committee of the Union.

10. The hon. secretary shall convene a special general meeting at any time on receiving a requisition to that effect signed by the secretaries of not less than forty dubs belonging to the Union, and stating specific notice of motion.

In case of a special general meeting, such must be held within one month of receipt of requisition, preliminary notice must be sent out by the hon. secretary within ten days of such requisition, and notices of amendment must be received by him within seventeen days of receipt of requisition.

11. That no bye-law, law of the game, or rule as to professionalism shall be altered, rescinded, or added to, without the consent of at least two-thirds of those present at a general meeting.

12. Each club shall be furnished with a copy of the bye-laws, laws of the game, and rules as to professionalism, and be bound thereby. In case of infringement thereof by any club or player, such club or player may be punished or expelled by the committee, subject to appeal to a general meeting, except on a matter of fact, when there shall not be any right of appeal.

13. Notice of any amendment or alteration in the byelaws, laws of the game, or rules as to professionalism, together

with the names of the proposing and seconding clubs, shall be given in writing to the hon. secretary, not later than August 7, a copy of such notice shall be sent to each club not later than August 14; and notice of any amendment to such amendment or alteration must be in writing signed by an official of the club making it, and must reach the hon. secretary by August 21, after which each club shall be advised by circular of the date of the annual general meeting, and of all proposed alterations and amendments.

14. The committee shall have sole control of the funds of the Union. The accounts shall be audited by two auditors, appointed at the previous annual general meeting. A printed copy of the signed balance-sheet shall be sent to each club, along with the notice calling the annual general meeting.

15. The committee may at any time before the end of July alter the distribution of the twenty seats; in case such re-distribution be challenged by any county, university, or district, the next annual general meeting shall be asked to confirm or reject such alteration on the vote of a majority.

16. The committee shall appoint three trustees, in whose names they may from time to time invest any funds of the Union; which investment shall be held by the said trustees solely for the furtherance of amateur Rugby football.

17. Any league or combination of clubs shall be under the authority of and shall obtain the consent of the Union to its formation, and shall be required to submit its proposed rules, and any subsequent alterations thereof, for approval to the Rugby Union committee, who shall have power –

(a) To forbid the formation or continuance of such league or combination of clubs in their absolute discretion.

(b) To discharge from membership or suspend any club contravening this bye-law.

(c) To suspend any club which shall play a match with a club which has been suspended or discharged from membership under the bye-law, or with any club which has been formed out of the nucleus of any suspended club.

18. In case any difference of opinion arises as to the meaning of any of these bye-laws, such meaning shall be decided by the committee, or, if it occurs at a general meeting, by the chairman thereof; any such decision shall be recorded in the minutes, and shall be accepted as the true meaning of the bye-law until otherwise interpreted at a general meeting, after due notice has been given.

Laws of the Game of Football, as Played by the Rugby Football Union

INTRODUCTION

1. The Rugby Game of Football should be played by fifteen players on each side. (Any one coming under the laws of professionalism shall not be allowed to take part in any game under this Union's jurisdiction.) The field of play shall not exceed no yards in length, nor 75 in breadth, and shall be as near these dimensions as practicable. The lines defining the boundary of the field of play shall be suitably marked, and shall be called the goal-lines at the ends and the; touch-lines at the sides. On each goal-line and equidistant from the touch-lines shall be two upright posts, called goal-posts, exceeding 11 ft. in height, and placed 18 ft. 6 in. apart, and joined by a cross-bar 10 ft. from the ground; and the object of the game shall be to kick the ball over this cross-bar and between the posts. The game shall be played with an oval ball of as nearly as possible the following size and weight, namely—

Length   11 to 11½ in.
Length circumference 30 to 31 in.
Width circumference 25½ to 26 in.
Weight   13 to 14½ in.
Hand-sewn and not less than eight stitches to the inch.

GLOSSARY, DUTIES OF OFFICIALS, SCORING

Glossary of Terms

The following terms occur in the laws, and have the respective meanings attached to each:

Dead-ball Line. Not more than 25 yards behind, and equidistant from the respective goal-lines, and parallel thereto, shall be lines, which shall be called the Dead-ball Lines, and if the ball or player holding the ball touch or cross these lines the ball shall be dead and out of play.

In-Goal. Those portions of the ground immediately at the ends of the field of play and between the touch-lines, produced to the dead-ball lines, are called In-goal. The goal-lines are in-goal.

Touch. Those portions of the ground immediately at the sides of the field of play and between the goal-lines, if produced, are called Touch. The touch-lines and all posts and flags marking these lines, or the centre, or 25 yards lines, are in touch.

Touch-in-Goal. Those portions of the ground immediately at the four corners of the field of play, and between the goal and touch-lines, if respectively produced, are called Touch-in-Goal. The corner posts and flags are in touch-in-goal.

A Drop-kick is made by letting the ball fall from the hands, and kicking it the very instant it rises.

A Place-kick is made by kicking the ball after it has been placed on the ground.

A Punt is made by letting the ball fall from the hands and kicking it before it touches the ground.

A Tackle is when the holder of the ball is held by one or more players of the opposite side.

A Scrummage, which can only take place in the field of play, is when the ball is put down between players who have closed round on their respective sides, and who must have both feet on the ground.

A Try is gained by the player who first puts his hand on the ball on the ground in his opponents' in-goal.

A Touch-down is when a player touches down as above in his own in-goal.

A Goal is obtained by kicking the ball from the field of play, except from a punt, from a kick-off, or from a drop-out, direct (i.e. without touching the ground or any player of either side) over the opponents' cross-bar, whether it touch such cross-bar or the goal-posts or not.

Knocking-on and Throwing-forward are propelling the ball by the hand or arm in the direction of the opponents' in-goal; a throw out of touch cannot be claimed as a throw-forward.

A Fair catch is a catch made direct from a kick or knock-on or throw-forward by one of the opposite side; the catcher must immediately claim the same by making a mark with his heel at the spot where he made the catch.

Kick-off is a place-kick from the centre of the field-of-play; the opposite side may not stand within ten yards of the ball, nor charge until the ball be kicked, otherwise another kick-off shall be allowed. If the ball pitch in touch, the opposite side may have it kicked off again.

Drop-out is a drop-kick from within 25 yards of the kicker's goal-line; within which distance the opposite side may not charge, otherwise another drop-out shall be allowed. If the ball pitch is in touch, the opposite side may have it dropped out again.

At kick-off the ball must reach the limit of ten yards, and at drop-out must reach the 25 yards line. If otherwise, the opposite side may have the ball re-kicked, or scrummaged, at the centre or in the middle of the 25 yards line, as the case may be.

Off-side.—See Laws 7 and 8.

Referee and Touch-judges
3. In all matches a Referee and two Touch-judges must be appointed, the former being mutually agreed upon. The Referee must carry a whistle, which he must blow in the following cases:

Duties of Referee
(a) When a player makes and claims a fair catch.
(b) When he notices rough or foul play or misconduct. For the first offence he shall either caution the player or order him off the ground, but for the second offence he must order him off. If ordered off, the player must be reported by him to this Union.
(c) When he considers that the continuation of play is dangerous.
(d) When the ball has been improperly put into a scrummage.
(e) When he wishes to stop the game for any purpose.
(f) If the ball or a player running with the ball touch him.

(g) At half-time and no-side, he being the sole timekeeper, having sole power to allow extra time for delays, but he shall not whistle for half-time or no-side until the ball be held or out of play.

(h) When a player in a scrummage lifts a foot from the ground before the ball has been put fairly into the scrummage.

(i) When he notices any irregularity of play whereby the side committing such gain an advantage.

(j) When he notices a breach of Laws 5 and 15.

Powers of Referee

The Referee shall be sole judge in all matters of fact, but as to matters of law there shall be the right of appeal to the Rugby Union.

Duty of Touch-judges

The touch-judges shall carry flags, and shall each take one side of the ground, outside the field of play, and the duty of each shall be to hold up his flag when and where the ball goes into touch, and also to assist the Referee, if requested by him, at kicks at goal.

Rules

4. The captains of the respective sides shall toss up for the choice of in-goal or the kick-off. Each side shall play an equal time from each in-goal, and a match shall be won by a majority of points; if no point be scored, or the number be equal, the match shall be drawn.

Scoring

The following shall be the mode of scoring

A Try	equals 3 points
A Penalty Goal	equals 3 points
A Goal from a Try	equals 5 points
(in which case the Try shall not count)	

Any other Goal   equals 4 points

Kick-off

5. At the time of the kick-off all the kicker's side shall be behind the ball; if any are in front, the Referee shall blow his whistle and order a scrummage where the kick-off took place. The game shall be re-started by a kick-off—

(a) After a goal, by the side losing such goal, and

(b) After half-time, by the opposite side to that which stated the game.

MODE OF PLAY, DEFINITIONS

Mode of Play

6. When once the game is started, the ball may be kicked or picked up and run with by any player who is on-side, at any time; except that it may not be picked up—

(a) In a scrummage.

(b) When it has been put down after it has been fairly held.

(c) When it is on the ground after a player has been tackled.
     It may be passed or knocked from one player to another, provided it be not passed, knocked, or thrown forward. If a player while holding or running with the ball be tackled and the ball fairly held, he MUST at once put it fairly down between him and his opponents' goal-line.

Off-side

7. A player is placed off-side if he enters a scrummage from his opponents' side, or if the ball has been kicked, touched, or is being run with by one of his own side behind him. A player can be off-side in his opponents' in-goal, but not in his own, except where one of his side takes a free kick behind his goal-line, in which case all his side must be behind the ball when kicked.

8. An off-side player is placed on-side—

(a) When an opponent has run five yards with the ball.

(b) When the ball has been kicked by, or has touched an opponent.

(c) When one of his side has run in front of him with the ball.

(d) When one of his side has run in front of him, having kicked the ball when behind him.

An off-side player shall not play the ball, nor during the time an opponent has the ball, run, tackle, or actively or passively obstruct, nor may he approach within ten yards of any player waiting for the ball. On any breach of this law, the opposite side shall be awarded, at their option—

(e) A free kick, the place of such breach being taken as the mark.

(f) A scrummage at the spot where the ball was last played by the offending side before such breach occurred.

Except in the case of unintentional off-side, when a scrummage shall be formed where such breach occurred.

Fair Catch

9. If a player makes a fair catch he shall be awarded a free kick, even though the whistle has been blown for a knock-on, and he himself must either kick or place the ball.

Free Kicks

10. All free kicks may be place-kicks, drop-kicks, or punts, but must be in the direction of the opponents' goal-line, and across the kicker's goal-line, if kicked from behind the same. They may be taken at any spot behind the mark in a line parallel to the touch-lines. If taken by drop or punt, the catcher must take the kick; if taken by a place-kick, the catcher must place the ball. In all cases the kicker's side must be behind the ball when it is kicked, except the player who may be placing the ball for a place-kick. In case of any

infringement of this law, the Referee shall order a scrummage at the mark. The opposite side may come up-to, and charge from anywhere on or behind a line drawn through the mark and parallel to the goal-lines, and may charge as soon as the catcher commences to run or offers to kick or places the ball on the ground for a place-kick, but in case of a drop-kick or punt, the kicker may always draw back, and unless he has dropped the ball, the opposite side must retire to the line of the mark. But if any of the opposite side do charge before the player having the ball commences to run or offers to kick, or the ball has touched the ground for a place-kick (and this applies to tries at goal as well as free kicks), provided the kicker has not taken his kick, the charge may be disallowed.

PENALTIES

Penalty Kicks for Intentionally Handling Ball or Falling in Scrummage.

11. Free kicks by way of penalties shall be awarded on claims by the opposite side, if any player—

(a) Intentionally either handles the ball, or falls down in a scrummage, or picks the ball out of a scrummage.

Not putting Ball down when held.

(b) Having the ball, does not immediately put it down in front of him on it being held.

Not getting up or allowing to get up.

(c) Being on the ground, does not immediately get up.

(d) Prevents an opponent getting up.

Illegally Obstructing, etc.

(e) Illegally tackles, charges, or obstructs, as in Law 8.

Unfairly putting Ball down.

(f) Wilfully puts the ball unfairly into a scrummage, or, the ball having come out, wilfully shoves it forward with his hands again into the scrummage.

Illegal Charge.

(g) Not himself running at the ball, charges or obstructs an opponent not holding the ball.

(h) Not in a scrummage wilfully obstructs his opponents' backs by standing on his opponents' side of the ball when it is in a scrummage.

(i) Being in a scrummage, lifts a foot from the ground before the ball has been put into such scrummage.

(j) Wilfully prevents the ball being fairly put into a scrummage.

The places of infringement shall be taken as the mark, and any one of the side granted the free kick may place or kick the ball.

GENERAL

Ball in Touch

12. The ball is in touch when it, or a player carrying it, touch or cross the touch-line; it shall then belong to the side opposite to that last touching it in the field of play, except when carried in. One of the side to whom the ball belongs shall bring it into play at the spot where it went into touch, by one of the following methods: –

(a) Bounding it on the field of play at right angles to the touch-line. After bounding it he may catch it, and then run with it, kick it, or pass it. When catching it he must have both feet in the field of play.

Throw-out

(a) Throwing it out so as to alight at right angles to the touch-line, or

(b) Scrummaging it at any spot at right angles to the touch-line, between 5 and 15 yards from the place where it went into touch.

(c) If the ball be not thrown out of touch, so as to alight at right angles to the touch-line, the opposite side may bring it out as in (c).

Try at Goal

12. When the side has scored a try, the ball shall be brought from the spot where the try was gained into the field of play in a line parallel to the touch-lines, such distance as the placer thinks proper, and there he shall place the ball for one of his side to try and kick a goal; this place-kick is governed by Law 10 as to charging, etc., the mark being taken as on the goal-line. It is the duty of the defending side to see that the ball is taken out straight.

Unfair Play, Allowing or Disallowing a Try

13. The Referee shall award a try, if, in his opinion, one would undoubtedly have been obtained but for unfair play or interference of the defending side. Or, he shall disallow a try, and adjudge a touch-down, if, in his opinion, a try would undoubtedly not have been gained but for unfair play or interference of the attacking side. In case of a try so allowed, the kick at goal shall be taken at any point on a line parallel to the touch-lines, and passing through the spot where the ball was when such unfair play or interference took place.

Ball Held in In-goal

14. If the ball, when over the goal-line and in possession of a player, be fairly held by an opposing player before it is grounded, it shall be scrummaged 5 yards from the goal-line, opposite the spot where the ball was held.

Drop-out

15. After an unsuccessful try or touch-down, or if the ball after crossing the goal-line go into touch-in-goal or touch,

or cross the dead-ball line, it shall be brought into play by means of a drop-out, when all the kicker's side must be behind the ball when kicked; in case any are in front, the Referee shall order a scrummage on the 25 yards line, and equi-distant from the touch-lines.

Knock-on, Throw-forward

16. In case of a throw-forward or knock-on, the ball shall be at once brought back to where such infringement took place, and there put down, unless a fair catch has been made and claimed, or unless the opposite side gain an advantage. If the ball or a player running with the ball touches the Referee, it shall there be put down.

Pass or Carry Back over Own Goal-line

17. If a player shall wilfully kick, pass, knock, or carry the ball back across his goal-line, and it there be made dead, the opposite side may claim that the ball shall be brought back, and a scrummage formed at the spot whence it was kicked, passed, knocked, or carried back. Under any other circumstances a player may touch the ball down in his own in-goal.

Hacking, Tripping

18. No hacking, or hacking over or tripping up, shall be allowed under any circumstances. No one wearing projecting nails, iron plates, or gutta-percha on any part of his boots or shoes shall be allowed to play in a match.

Irregularities in In-Goal Not Otherwise Provided For

19. In case of any law being infringed in in-goal by the attacking side, a touch-down shall be awarded, but where such breach is committed by the defending side, a scrummage shall be awarded 5 yards from the goal-line, opposite to the spot where the breach occurred.

Other Irregularities Not Provided For

But in the case of any law being broken, or any irregularity of play occurring on the part of either side not otherwise provided for, the ball shall be taken back to the place where the breach of the law or irregularity of play occurred, and a scrummage formed there.

Close Time

20. There shall be an annual close time, during which it is illegal to play football where gate-money is taken, such close time being between April 20 and September 1.

REGULATIONS AUTHORIZED BY THE RUGBY UNION ON COUNTY QUALIFICATIONS.

1. A man may play –
   (a) For the county in which he was born, or
   (b) For the county in which he has resided for the six months previous to the time of playing, or
   (c) For the county in which he is residing at school or college, either as pupil or master, at the time of playing, provided his residence at the school or college be in the same county.
   (d) For the county for which he played in season 1887–1888.

2. A man shall still be qualified to play for a county, having previously qualified for and played for that county for three seasons, and not having subsequently played for any other county.
3. No man shall play for more than one county during the same season.
4. A man who is duly qualified and plays for a county in a certain season, may continue to play for that county

during the remainder of that season, even though he loses his other qualifications.

5. Should any question arise as to qualifications, the same shall be left to the decision .of the Rugby Union Committee.

RULES AS TO PROFESSIONALISM

Adopted at Rugby Union Meeting, September, 1895, which shall take the place of the Rules as to Professionalism, the "Insurance Laws," and the "Transfer Laws," which were in operation previously.

1. Professionalism is illegal.

2. Acts of professionalism are:
(1) By an individual—
A. Asking, receiving, or relying on a promise, direct or implied, to receive any money consideration whatever, actual or prospective; any employment or advancement; any establishment in business; or any compensation whatever for—
  (a) Playing football, or rendering any service to a football organization.
  (b) Training, or loss of time connected therewith.
  (c) Time lost in playing football or in travelling in connection with football.
  (d) Expenses in excess of the amount actually disbursed on account of reasonable hotel or travelling expenses.
B. Transferring his services from one club to another in opposition to Rule 6.
C. Playing for a club while receiving, or after having received from such club, any consideration whatever for acting as secretary, treasurer, or in any other office, or for doing

or for having done any work or labour about the club's ground or in connection with the club's affairs.

D. Remaining on tour at his club's expense longer than is reasonable.

E. Giving or receiving any money testimonial. Or giving or receiving any other testimonial, except under the authority of this Union.

F. Receiving any medal or other prize for any competition except under the authority of this Union.

G. Playing on any ground where gate-money is taken:

(a) During the close season.

(b) In any match or contest where it is previously agreed that less than fifteen players on each side shall take part.

H. Knowingly playing with or against any expelled or suspended player or club.

I. Refusing to give evidence or otherwise assist in carrying out these rules when requested by this Union to do so.

J. Being registered as, or declared a professional, or suspended by any National Rugby Union, or by the Football Association.

K. Playing within eight days of any accident for which he has claimed or received insurance compensation, if insured under these rules.

L. Playing in any benefit match connected directly or indirectly with football.

M. Knowingly playing or acting as referee or touch-judge on the ground of an expelled or suspended club.

(2) By a club or other organization:

A. Paying or promising payment, or giving, offering, or promising any inducement as to employment, advancement, or establishment in business, or any compensation whatever to any player for—

(a) Playing for that club.

(b) Training, or for travelling expenses to or from any training resort, or for loss of time in connection with training.

(c) Loss of time while playing or travelling in connection with football.

(d) Hotel or travelling expenses in excess of the sum actually and reasonably disbursed.

B. Receiving as a member a member of another club in opposition to Rule 6.

C. Receiving or continuing as a member any one it may pay or have paid for either regular or occasional services.

D. Paying for any of its teams, players, officials, or members on tour longer than a reasonable time; or paying for more than a reasonable number.

E. Giving from its funds, subscribing, or playing a match for any testimonial.

F. Giving any medal or other prize for any competition except under the authority of this Union.

G. Taking gate-money at any ground –

(a) During the close season.

(b) At any match or contest where it is previously agreed that less than fifteen players on each side shall take part.

H. Knowingly playing or allowing its members to play with or against any expelled or suspended player or club.

I.   Refusing to produce its books or documents, or to allow its officials or members to give evidence, or to assist in carrying out these rules when requested by the Union to do so.

J.   Knowingly playing or admitting as a member, without the consent of the Union, any member or an expelled or suspended club, or any expelled or suspended player, or any person registered as or declared a professional or suspended by any National Rugby Union or by the Football Association.

K. Knowingly allowing a player to play in its matches within eight days of any accident for which he has received or claimed insurance compensation, if insured under these rules.

L. Playing or allowing its ground to be used for any benefit match connected directly or indirectly with football.

M. Knowingly allowing its members or teams to play on the ground of any expelled or suspended club.

N. Refusing to pay, within one month, any costs or expenses ordered by this Union for inquiries held under these rules.

3. For offences under 2 (1), A, H, I, L, and M, an individual shall be expelled from all English clubs playing Rugby football, and shall not be eligible for re-election or election to any club. For offences under 2 (1), B, C, D, E, F, G, J, and K, an individual shall be suspended during the pleasure of this Union.

4. For offences under 2 (2), A, D, H, I, L, M, and N, a club shall be expelled from this Union. For offences under 2 (2), B, C, E, F, G, J, and K, a club shall be suspended during the pleasure of this Union. Any club disregarding a sentence of suspension shall be liable to expulsion.

5. When this Union is fully satisfied that any offence under 2 (2), A, D, H, I, L, M, and N, was of an accidental, trivial, or technical character, they may suspend instead of expel.

6. When a player wishes to join a new club he may do so; if this Union request it, he shall produce a letter from his old

club stating that they have no objection; on receipt of such letter this Union shall give the necessary permission, unless they believe there may have been collusion, or that illegal means have been employed to induce the player to join the new club, in which case they shall hold an inquiry. In case any club or clubs refuse to give such written permission, this Union must hold an inquiry, at the request of the player or of the club he wishes to join. If from any cause an inquiry be held, this Union shall have full power to order the payment of the costs of such inquiry, and of the clubs and witnesses, as it may think fit.

This Union may grant power to recognized governing bodies to increase the stringency of this rule, provided such proposed alterations be submitted to and approved of by it.

7. A county or club may insure its players either through –
A. A recognized insurance company, or
B. A fund entirely set apart for insurance; the accounts of such fund to be yearly audited by a professional auditor. Such audit to be made at the close of each season, and to be concluded, and the auditor's certificate lodged with this Union, not later than May 20 in each year, provided that:

(a) Any injured player does not receive more than 6s per week-day while injured.
(b) Payments are only made on the certificate of a registered medical practitioner.
(c) Any player does not play football within eight days of his accident. If he does so, no insurance compensation shall be paid.
(d) Proper books of accounts be kept.

8. This Union may hold inquiries into any alleged breaches of these rules at its pleasure, and shall do so

when requested by any club or member of a club, provided any such club or member make a preliminary deposit of £10, or such smaller sum as this Union may determine, to be accompanied by a preliminary written statement of the chief known facts. After any such inquiry, this Union may return the preliminary deposit, wholly or in part, and may order the expenses of such inquiry, of clubs and members implicated, and of witnesses, to be paid as it may determine.

9. At all inquiries under Rules 6 and 8 correct notes must be taken.

10. Any club, member, or player affected by any decision given by a county, union of counties, or university, under delegation of powers contained in Rule 11, may appeal direct to this Union. Such appeal must be made within ten days, and must be accompanied by a deposit of £50 and a written statement of the grounds of appeal. After any such appeal, this Union may return such deposit, wholly or in part, and may order the expenses of such inquiry, of club and members implicated, and of witnesses, to be paid as it may determine.

11. This Union may delegate to recognized governing bodies, such as counties, union of counties, and universities, powers to act for it in such cases and under such regulations as it may determine. All powers so delegated, and the bodies to whom such delegation be made, shall be published annually in the official guide of this Union.

12. This Union may appoint a sub-committee or committees to act on its behalf in all cases arising under these rules, giving such powers as it may determine.

13. This Union shall have power to deal with all acts which it may consider as acts of professionalism, and which are not specifically provided for.

14. Where the word "Union" is used in these rules, the committee of this Union for the time being shall be understood, and, in the delegation of powers, the committee of the recognized governing body shall be understood. In case any difference of opinion arises as to the meaning of any of these rules, such meaning shall be decided by the committee of this Union, or, if it occurs at a general meeting, by the chairman thereof. Any such decision shall be entered in the minutes, and shall be accepted as the true meaning until otherwise interpreted by a two-thirds majority at a general meeting of this Union after due notice has been given.

DELEGATION OF POWERS

The Rugby Union Committee have delegated to the following recognized governing bodies, namely, to the counties of Northumberland, Durham, Cumberland, Westmorland, Yorkshire, Lancashire, Cheshire, Middlesex, Kent, Surrey, Sussex, Hampshire, Gloucestershire, Somersetshire, Devonshire, and Cornwall; to the Universities of Oxford and Cambridge; to the Midland Counties' and Eastern Counties' Unions; and to the Northern Federation (consisting of the counties of Northumberland, Durham, Cumberland and Westmorland, for any cases not exclusively in one of these counties, but within two or more of the four). The following powers to act for them, namely:

A.—Under Rule II in the Rules as to Professionalism.

Under Rules 2, 3, and 4 all powers except—

(1) The power of reinstatement after suspension.

(2) The passing of sentence of expulsion.

If individuals or clubs are found guilty under 2 (1) A, H, J, L, or M, or 2 (2) A, H, J, L, M, or N, they must be at once temporarily suspended, and reported to the Rugby Union. Under Rules 6, 7, and 8 all powers.

The Rugby Union Committee solely have the power of expelling. The Rugby Union Committee also solely have the power to reinstate after suspension.

B.—*Under the Laws of the Game*, the following powers: Law 3 (b).

The above powers are only delegated to recognized governing bodies, when all individuals and clubs involved are under the jurisdiction of one governing body.

While delegating the above powers, the Rugby Union Committee wish it to be distinctly understood that the above recognized governing bodies have not the power or right to further delegate any of these powers.

The Rugby Union Committee have ruled that where the words "expelled or suspended club or player," or words to this effect, are used in the Rules as to Professionalism, they shall be read to include any professional club or player.

The Committee wish to specially draw the attention of county and club committees to the fact that recognized governing bodies have no power to sanction the formation of Leagues, or combination of clubs, and also to the alterations in bye-law 17, as to Leagues having to submit any alteration in or addition to their Laws or Rules, to this Union, and as to the power of this Union to forbid the continuance of any League.

The Committee have delegated to the New Zealand Union the power to carry out their regulations, and have given them the right to delegate such powers to other Bodies in New Zealand by means of a match between the two counties at the head of the Northern and Southern Groups respectively.

4. Each match shall be decided by points. A win shall score two points, and a drawn game one point to each side. If in any case, owing to two or more counties scoring an equal number of points, a winner is not ascertained, the Rugby Football Union Committee may declare the winner, or, in their discretion, order another match or matches to be played.

5. The matches referred to in Regulation 2 (II.), (a), (b), (c), and (d) must be played by January 20; and the matches referred to in Regulation 2 (I.) and (II.) (e), must be played by February 20; the date of the match for the Championship shall be fixed by the Rugby Football Union Committee should the two counties interested fail to agree.

6. The match for the Championship shall be played in the North of England, if North *v*. South has been played in the South, and vice versa; the home county having choice of ground. The net proceeds of the match shall be equally divided between the two counties engaged.

7. Regulation 1 shall not be varied except by the vote of a General Meeting.

8. Any question which shall arise and is not above provided for, may be decided by the Rugby Football Union Committee.

9. That the Rugby Union Committee may delegate to a Sub-Committee of their Body the exercise of all or any of the powers conferred on them by the above regulations.

BYE-LAWS OF THE INTERNATIONAL RUGBY FOOTBALL BOARD

1. The Board shall be called "The International Rugby Football Board."

2. The Board shall consist of twelve representatives—six from the Rugby Union, and two from each of the other Unions. The chairman, who shall have a casting vote, shall be appointed at each meeting, in regular rotation from the different Unions in their order of seniority.

3. The Board shall meet annually at Manchester, or at such place as is agreed upon by all the Unions, in the third week of October in each year.

4. All international matches shall be played under the laws approved of by this Board.

5. In case of disputes in international matches, a committee of the Board, consisting of two representatives appointed by each Union, shall have absolute and exclusive jurisdiction. The Board shall have no power to interfere with the game as played within the limits of the different Unions.

6. Notice of any proposed alteration in the laws of the game, or in the bye-laws of the Board, shall be sent to the hon. sec. at least four weeks before the annual meeting in October, and the hon. sec. shall intimate these proposals to the Unions at least three weeks before the meeting.

7. The hon. sec. shall at any time convene a special meeting of the Board on receipt of a requisition from the hon. secs, of at least two of the Unions. The purpose for which the

meeting is desired shall be intimated to the different Unions at least three weeks before the said meeting.

8. If the chairman entitled for the time being to preside shall on the occasion of any appeal happen to be a representative of either of the disputing Unions, his chairmanship shall be postponed in favour of, and take order next after, the chairmanship of the first neutral Union entitled by rotation to furnish a chairman.

9. The Referee at any match shall be ineligible to act as a representative at the meeting called to settle any dispute arising out of that match.

10. No alteration in the laws of the game or the bye-laws of the Board shall be made at any meeting called for that purpose, unless by a majority of at least three-fourths of the representatives present.

11. All expenses incurred in connection with the Board shall be equally defrayed by the Unions; but in the case of a committee appointed under Bye-law 5, all hotel and travelling expenses shall be equally defrayed by the disputing Unions.

12. All decisions of the Board or committee shall be accepted as final.

NATIONAL QUALIFICATION

There is no definition controlling any player's choice as to the country for which he shall play. The International Board in 1894 decided, at Leeds, that no player should in future play for more than one country, but did not proceed further.